SandScript

A Journal of Contemporary Writing

Volume II
2004

Emerald Coast Writers

2nd Annual
Writers' Conference

February 3-5, 2005

Ramada Beach Resort
Fort Walton Beach, Florida

Early Registration and Welcome Reception
on Thursday, *plus*
Two full days and nights!

Keynote Speaker: James W. Hall

Meet Editors, Agents,
Published Writers, Aspiring Writers

Workshops
Discussion Panels
Book Signings
Announcement of Contest Winners
for *SandScript, Volume III*

Full details and registration information
can be found on our website:
www.emeraldcoastwriters.org

Emerald Coast Writers

Words are things; and a small drop of ink
Falling like dew upon a thought, produces
That which makes thousands,
                perhaps millions, think.

-Lord Byron, poet (1788-1824)

SandScript

A Journal of Contemporary Writing

Volume II

2004

Emerald Coast Writers

POBox 6502, Destin, Florida 32550
www.emeraldcoastwriters.org

Support for *SandScript* and Emerald Coast Writers, Inc. (ECW) is provided by the generosity of our members, gifts and charitable contributions from individual readers, friends and the area businesses listed in this journal. Tax-deductible contributions are acknowledged herein.

ECW membership is open to anyone; however, membership greatly benefits writers living along or having connections to Florida's Northwest Gulf Coast. Membership information is posted online at: www.emeraldcoastwriters.org.

SandScript is a yearly publication of Emerald Coast Writers, Inc., a non-profit literary organization, P.O. Box 6502, Destin, FL 32550. Order online at www.emeraldcoastwriters.org or by mail. Single copy rate: $10.00, plus $3.50 shipping and handling.

Submissions:
The literary works in *SandScript* are published as a result of Emerald Coast Writers' yearly literary contest. Contest dates, submission information and guidelines can be found online at: www.emeraldcoastwriters.org

Advertising and sponsorships:
Full page and half page ads are available in future editions of *SandScript*. Sponsorships are also accepted on our website. Exchange proposals considered. Write or email for rates.

Permissions:
Authors in *SandScript* hold the rights to their individual works and should be contacted directly. Emerald Coast Writers, Inc. may be able to assist in locating these authors.

Distribution:
Bookstores can purchase *SandScript* through Ingram Books, 1226 Heil Quaker Blvd., LaVergne, TN 37086.

International Standard Serial Number (ISSN#) 1543-3846
ISBN# 0-9742186-1-8
©2004 by Emerald Coast Writers, Inc. All rights reserved.

Cover Art © 2004 by Loretta Menendian. All rights reserved.

SandScript
A Journal of Contemporary Writing

Volume II
2004

Published yearly by Emerald Coast Writers, Inc., a non-profit literary organization for writers.

P.O. Box 6502, Destin, FL 32550
www.emeraldcoastwriters.org

Publisher/Managing Editor
Darlene Dean

Copy Editor
Sherry Marcolongo

Contest Coordinator
Tom Corcoran

Advisors
Lynne Christen
Diane Harris
Joyce Holland
Janet Manchon

Ellen Martin
Delores Merrill
Julia Schuster
Phil Turner

Judges
John Dufresne
Denise Duhamal
Linda Evanchyk

Dr. Vicki Hunt
Delores Merrill

Cover Artist
Loretta Menendian

SandScript
A Journal of Contemporary Writing - Volume II

Acknowledgments

The Board of Directors and members of Emerald Coast Writers, Inc., would like to thank the following contributors, sponsors and friends for their support in the publication of this journal.

Cover Art
Artist Loretta Menendian has over 20 years of professional experience in artistic design and commercial fine art. She is a current resident of Florida's Emerald Coast, has owned her own businesses for several years and has had her work exhibited in numerous public showings. Ms. Menendian is currently an art instructor in the local area.

Special Feature Story by Jeremiah Healy
"Habits" has been graciously provided by Jeremiah Healy. Boston-lawyer-turned-writer, he also writes as Terry Devane, and has over 16 novels and 60 short stories published. He has received several awards and is a frequent speaker around the world on the art of writing mysteries.

Special Feature Story by Julia Schuster
A shorter version of "Fruitcake Cookies and Bringing Mother Back to Life" is soon to be published as "The Trouble with Fruitcake," in A Cup of Comfort for Sisters (Oct 2004, ISBN #1-59337-097-0). The story is printed here in its entirety with full permission from the author and Adams Media, F+W Publications.

The worth of a book is to be measured by what you can carry away from it.
James Bryce

Judges

John Dufresne – *Short Fiction*

John Dufresne grew up in Massachusetts and attended Worcester State College and the MFA program in creative writing at the University of Arkansas. He teaches in the Creative Writing Program at Florida International University, and lives in Dania Beach, Florida.

Dufresne's most recent publication, *The Lie That Tells a Truth* (W.W. Norton & Company, 2003), is a book on fiction writing. He is also the author of the story collection, *The Way That Water Enters Stone* (W.W. Norton & Company, 1991). His novel *Louisiana Power & Light* (W.W. Norton & Company, 1994) was a Barnes & Noble Discover Great New Writers selection. It was also a New York Times Notable Book of the Year, as was his second novel, *Love Warps the Mind a Little* ((W.W. Norton & Company, 1997). His most recent novel is *Deep in the Shade of Paradise* (W.W. Norton & Company, 2002). Many of his books were subsequently printed by Plume Books in paperback.

Denise Duhamal – *Poetry*

Denise Duhamel teaches creative writing and literature at Florida International University and lives in Hollywood, FL. Her most recent poetry title is *Queen for a Day: Selected and New Poems* (University of Pittsburgh Press, 2001). Her other titles include *The Star-Spangled Banner,* winner of Crab Orchard Award in Poetry (Southern Illinois University Press, 1999), and *Kinky* a book of poems devoted to Barbie dolls (Orchises Press, 1997). She has read her work on National Public Radio and, in the fall of 1999, was a featured poet on the PBS special Bill Moyers "Fooling with Words." Duhamel was educated at Emerson College (BFA) and Sarah Lawrence College (MFA) and is a winner of a National Endowment for the Arts Fellowship.

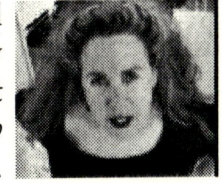

Judges (continued)

Linda Evanchyk – *Children's Fiction*

Linda Evanchyk is a journalism teacher at Choctawhatchee High School in Ft. Walton Beach, Florida. She was recently named a National Board Certified Teacher. She has been her school and school district's teacher of the year and also a Florida Journalism Teacher of the Year and a Dow Jones Newspaper Fund Distinguished National Adviser. Evanchyk has also won awards for her own writing including a Lantern Award of Excellence from the Southern Public Relations Foundation and an Award of Merit from the National Scholastic Public Relations Association. Her writing includes numerous articles for periodicals as well as material about her local area. In 2003, she had her first book released, which was written with a colleague. "Those Who Teach Do More: Tributes to American Teachers" features some 175 well-known Americans who submitted stories of a teacher who made a difference in their lives.

Dr. Vickie Hunt – *Non-fiction & Essay*

Vickie Hunt teaches creative writing at Okaloosa-Walton College and the University of West Florida. She received her Ph.D. from Florida State University. Her work has appeared in *The Chattahoochee Review, Apalachee Quarterly, Bomb Magazine,* and elsewhere, including the anthologies *Every Woman I've Ever Loved* and *His Hands, His Tools, His Sex, His Dress*.

Judges (continued)

Delores Busbee Merrill – *Short-Short Fiction & Plays*
Delores Merrill has an MFA in Theatre from the University of Alabama, and at present, she works as the House Manager for The Arts Center of Okaloosa-Walton College. Her plays have been produced for several different regional theatres including *Goodbye Lenore* (February 2004) for Cornerpocket Theatre in Niceville, FL. She was a finalist for the Eugene O'Neill Playwriting Award for her work *Vincent's Candle*.

Merrill conducts workshops on playwriting, acting and writing for the Readers Theatre. In addition, she has had theatre criticism papers workshopped at SETC and the National Speech Conference and published in the Alabama Arts Association Journal. Her poetry has been published in many publications including Southern university journals. For the past three years, Merrill's photography, combined with poetry, has been exhibited in the Holzhaur Art Gallery of the Okaloosa-Walton College.

A Letter from the President

I address you today from my new home office in Memphis. It's a little roomier than my "closet" office in Destin was, but oh, so far away from my beloved sugar-white beaches, and more importantly, all of you, my dear and cherished friends of Emerald Coast Writers. I've always loved the image of life as a book, a mystery, I think, where change is illustrated by the turning of a page. I've tried to live my life with all the expectation of an avid reader eager for the next conflict and determined to figure out each plot twist before the author or the last page beat me to it.

Moving has brought out the sentimental side of me it seems, and I find myself reflecting on where I have been, Chapters 1 through... well, let's just say the present, and where I am headed, or what awaits me at the next chapter break. This process could not be complete without including my Emerald Coast Writers memories and my hopes and dreams for its future success.

This relatively small literary organization has accomplished so much in its brief existence. *SandScript – Volume One* astonished us. We successfully conducted a literary competition, judged the entries and published a literary journal worthy of our pride.

Our first annual Emerald Coast Writers' Workshop last March surpassed all our expectations and taught us that the writers along Florida's Northwest Gulf Coast expect and appreciate our promise to deliver a top-notch conference each year. Plans for the 2005 conference are well underway. Where will you be in February 2005? I know I'll be back on the Emerald Coast. I've already booked my trip.

At the Arts Center at Okaloosa-Walton College, our monthly meetings offer area writers a wide range of professional and informative speakers and an opportunity to network with other writers. Writing is a solitary endeavor, however being published requires having lots and lots of friends.

SandPrints, our quarterly newsletter, unfolded slowly; but it has evolved into a lively and informative publication enjoyed by our members and sponsors alike.

Membership doubled after our last SandScript competition and continues to flourish; however, with that blessing comes the added responsibility to meet the needs of so many. I am pleased and thankful for the members who have stepped forward to volunteer for board positions and committee posts that had once been held by a very few dedicated visionaries. There is still much to do, and it is paramount that each of you step up and contribute your much needed talents. After all, giving to a cause you believe in is the greatest gift you can give yourself.

And here we have *SandScript - Volume II*. Is there any limit to the literary talent of writers along the Emerald Coast? I think not. Within these pages of this second volume of *SandScript*, readers will discover a literary wellspring of creativity spanning every genre. Our team of dedicated judges and editors took on the challenge to improve upon the original and succeeded by compiling an exceptional publication. I thank them all for their efforts and their hours and hours of hard work. To the authors represented here: Thank you and well done!! Each winning entry is a literary jewel.

I savor each book I read, lock its essence in my heart, and then pass it on to a cherished friend, hoping that person, too, will discover its magic.

Likewise, I have savored each moment as president of Emerald Coast Writers. I grow and learn daily from its members and their creative essence. I am filled with joy and expectation as I pass the honor of being your president to another member of ECW who shares our vision for this group. New ideas and new faces are what keep us moving forward. I can't wait to see what happens next.

Respectfully,

Julia Horst Schuster
Founder and President 2000-2004
Emerald Coast Writers, Inc.

Writing is easy. All you do is sit staring at a blank sheet of paper until the drops of blood form on your forehead.
~ Gene Fowler

SandScript Contest Winners - 2004

Non-Fiction

First Place	"Pop Culture Revisited"	by Melita Gardner
Second Place	"On Belay with Johnny"	by Audrey Wendland
Third Place	"The Lean Acres Chronicles"	by Ronald H. Allen

Honorable Mention
"An Investigation of the Hermaphroditic Influence in *As You Like It* and *Cymbeline* on the Seventeenth Century Idea of Woman"
by Delores Merrill

Poetry

First Place	"Fear's Birth"	by Julia Schuster
Second Place	"November 22, 1963"	by Don Harrison
Third Place	"Winter Swamp"	by Reg Altazan

Honorable Mentions
"Friend" — by Darlene Dean
"Homeless" — by Darlene Dean
"Sonya Renay Was in the Paper" — by Delores Merrill

Short-Short Fiction

First Place	"Like Moses"	by Lou Krueger
Second Place	"Too Old"	by Jacqueline Bouchard
Third Place	"Last Thread"	by Reg Altazan

Honorable Mention
"A Cat's Tale" — by Melita Gardner

Short Fiction

First Place	"Justice Brings Me No Solace"	by Jacqueline Bouchard
Second Place	"That Palich Woman"	by Melita Gardner
Third Place	"Kareem's Roti"	by Ronald Frazer

Honorable Mention
"Drowning by Proxy" — by Melita Gardner

Children's Fiction

First Place	"Tigra's Quest"	by Ellen Martin
Second Place	"The Old Woman's Song"	by Riotta Scott
Third Place	"The Girl Who Was Afraid of Dogs"	by Natasha Santo

Honorable Mention
"Something's Under the Bed" — by Maureen Vreeland

Table of Contents

Conference 2005 Invitation .... *i*

SandScript Committee v

Acknowledgments vi

Judges vii

Letter from the President x

SandScript 2004 Winners xii

Winning Entries

Winter Swamp 1
    Reg Altazan, Third Place Poetry

Pop Culture Revisited 2
    Melita Gardner, First Place Non-Fiction

The Girl Who Was Afraid of Dogs 7
    Natasha Santo, Third Place Children's Fiction

That Palich Woman 9
    Melita Gardner, Second Place Short Fiction

Fear's Birth 17
    Julia Schuster, First Place Poetry

Justice Brings Me No Solace 18
    Jacqueline Bouchard, First Place Short Fiction

On Belay With Johnny 26
    Audrey Wendland, Second Place Non-Fiction

Friend 31
    Darlene Dean, Honorable Mention Poetry

Table of Contents *(continued)*

Tigra's Quest 32
    Ellen Martin, First Place Children's Fiction

Last Thread 40
    Reg Altazan, Third Place Short-Short Fiction

November 22, 1963 43
    Don Harrison, Second Place Poetry

Kareem's Roti 44
    Ronald Frazer, Third Place Short Fiction

Drowning by Proxy 51
    Melita Gardner, Honorable Mention Short Fiction

Like Moses 59
    Lou Krueger, First Place Short-Short Fiction

The Lean Acres Chronicles 63
    Ronald H. Allen, Third Place Non-Fiction

Homeless 70
    Darlene Dean, Honorable Mention Poetry

The Old Woman's Song 72
    Riotta Scott, Second Place Children's Fiction

Sonya Renay Was in the Paper 78
    Delores Merrill, Honorable Mention Poetry

A Cat's Tale 79
    Melita Gardner, Honorable Mention Short-Short Fiction

Too Old 83
    Jacqueline Bouchard, Second Place Short-Short Ficton

Something's Under the Bed 86
    Maureen Vreeland, Honorable Mention Children's Fiction

An Investigation of the Hermaphroditic Influence in *As You Like It* and *Cymbeline* on the Seventeenth Century Idea of Woman 88
    Delores Merrill, Honorable Mention Non-Fiction

Table of Contents *(continued)*

Special Contributions

A Word from the Publisher 96

Habits 97
    Jeremiah Healy, Short Story

Fruitcake Cookies and Bringing Mother Back to Life 106
    Julia Schuster, Non-Fiction

Indexes

ECW Membership Application 113

Emerald Coast Writers - Membership List 114

Emerald Coast Writers - Published Writers 116

Index of *SandScript* entries - by Author 121

All that mankind has done, thought, gained or been: it is lying as in magic preservation in the pages of books.
    — Thomas Carlyle

Emerald Coast Writers, Inc.
is a proud member of the:

Okaloosa Arts Alliance

※ ※ ※

REG ALTAZAN   SandScript 2004

WINTER SWAMP

Third Place Poetry

Cool, orange as a turtle eye,
evening sun soothes the skin
of winter sky,
hands down
a useless taste of light
to lifeless leaves,
stains the bones of cypress trees.

Hollow reeds, turned to glass,
shiver, snap in two,
drift in clouds at water's edge,
in shadows turn to blue.
Rusty ribbed cypress leaves
bump among cypress knees,
sink or float,
wrecks of tiny boats.

Snowy egrets stalk step,
pin point eyes drawn near
expanding rings of fat fish dreams
beneath an amber mirror.

MELITA GARDNER

POP CULTURE REVISITED

First Place Non-Fiction

When Elvis Presley first burst on the American scene, it was easy for me to ignore him, even laugh at him, because he represented something that was alien to me even though I had become an American citizen. But the impact he had on people was brought home to me on the day of his death. At that time I lived in Niceville, Florida, and was taking summer courses at the University of West Florida in Pensacola, so my friend Terry and I commuted four times a week. On August 16, 1977, we were on the road when we heard the news. All radio stations played his songs, and Terry wept all the way to the campus. When we arrived, the other students were crying, too. They put arms around each other and sang one of his songs after another, poignant, true and beautiful. I cried, too.

That incident opened my eyes to popular culture, that oxymoron to the "highbrow" intellectuals, who pretend they don't belong to "the masses." I realized then that popular culture, a product of popular imagination, bonds. Every country has such a culture — the tunes street urchins whistle, the music teenagers dance to, the fashions. Everywhere it appeals to young people, often inspiring rebelliousness, especially in countries ruled by oppressive governments, and even to snobs, if they are honest with themselves. Classical musicians go dancing, writers go to cafes to listen to popular music and even Prince Charles wears jeans. American "pop" culture, however, has had the widest influence the world over, in many countries the emblem of the hated or the admired "West."

When I was growing up in Zagreb, at that time a part of the communist Yugoslavia, gypsy music was our "pop." In our teens, my friends and I used to sneak into bars — a risky enterprise because if found out we could have been expelled from high school — to hear gypsy music. The biggest thrill was a swarthy violinist playing the ever-popular "Black Eyes," preferably for our table. We were young and sentimental and wore our hearts on our sleeves. I remember a young man who made violin strings weep when he serenaded us. My best friend fell in love with him, and I wrote a play dripping with melodrama about a girl in love with a mad violinist. After that, "cabaret" music, decadent and frowned upon by the communists, came in fashion. In the thirties, the Nazis had banned cabaret music because it was decadent, and Kurt Weil and Bertold Brecht, composer and writer of *The Three Penny Opera,* had to go into exile to the United States. Ironically, the Soviet Union branded the same kind of art as "capitalist." The fact that "decadent" music was allowed in Yugoslavia at all showed Yugoslavia was more progressive than other communist countries. Tito, after all, was the leader of the Third World, supposedly not aligned.

The genre officially encouraged, however, was opera, and it was hard to get tickets to any performance. In Zagreb, street urchins whistled arias from *Carmen*; a friend, an accomplished whistler, whistled "Toreador" to summon me from the house when I was grounded. We stalked singers and ballet dancers and collected their signatures.

But that was all juvenilia in comparison to the rage the movies became. James Mason was my idol: the dark, smoldering looks, big mouth, cruel eyes. The more melodramatic and sentimental the movie the better. I remember a scene in a James Mason film when he strikes his ward's hands with his cane. He is in love with her and she is trying to play the piano. The sadder the ending the better. In the Scandinavian film *She Danced One Summer,* young lovers, whose parents prevented them from seeing each other, died in a motorcycle accident, her arms around him, her head on his shoulder. I saw the film with a friend whose boyfriend had been killed the summer before in a mountain climbing accident on Black Mountain; I half expected Stanka to run out of the theatre and throw herself under the first street car clanking down the Ilitsa Street. Movies opened the door to the world outside, otherwise hidden from us or distorted by communist propaganda. It was good to see that young people in the West suffered as much "angst" as we did.

But it was the upbeat American movies, when they finally arrived in the early fifties, that became the real addiction and long lines formed before cash registers selling tickets for *An American in Paris.* America offered hope. Again, the fact that American movies were shown in Zagreb testified to Yugoslavia's mood at that time. American hits replaced "Oh, divine Aida" on the streets of my city. At about the same time, the true "pop" culture began creeping in. We danced the twist and listened to smuggled American jazz records on record players that had to be cranked up and would unwind to produce that quavering sound of a dying record. We heard Gershwin; his cult culminated in a performance of *Porgy and Bess* on the Zagreb stage: a real triumph for openness. Those of us who managed to get the tickets felt ourselves superior, truly "cool," even if we didn't know the word. Soon American icons like Joan Crawford and Bette Davis replaced Sartre, existentialism and philosophical discussions on street corners. It became "cool" to study English and talk about anything American. Lecture halls in the English department of the University of Zagreb became so crowded we had to take turns to go to classes. Profound philosophical discussions retreated into the less frequented halls of academia, which began publishing a magazine called *Praxis,* later an organ of young Croatian nationalists whose ideas fueled the Croatian separatist movement. But by then I was long gone.

Croatian dreams of America went beyond "pop." It was heroic to try to get a passport and leave the communist Yugoslavia. Getting a student visa was a feat. After I accomplished the impossible, I became a legend: the girl who got away. But once in America, I became wary of "pop" and was offended by vulgar displays. Ironically, I studied philosophy and discussed serious matters with the "squares" (not an "in" word yet).

My first encounter with "pop" as practiced in America was a political rally on the campus of the University of Washington in Seattle, where cheerleaders, clad in short skirts, leaped and waved pompons, shouting John F. Kennedy's name. For me politics was serious. In Yugoslavia, despite cultural openness, daring to speak up had bad consequences, like going to jail. Screaming a politician's name might have endangered his life. The kind of display I witnessed in 1960 was best left to movie or pop star fans, like those of Paul Anka, popular at that time. Girls screamed at his concerts, which I saw once or twice on the television screen at the Delta Zeta sorority where I was a guest.

Being a Delta Zeta exposed me to the real pop culture. At the house, every Friday night I watched television, something I had only heard about in Zagreb. I participated in the Saturday rituals of waiting for a date. We put our hair in curlers and listened to the telephone. The girl who was lucky enough to receive that magic call would scream and announce to everybody, "I got a date, I got a date." I never had a "steady," but I did go on a "blind" date my sorority sisters arranged for me. It was no different than sitting at a cafeteria table with a fellow student discussing a class assignment. I felt superior to such sophomoric displays and felt alienated from that popular culture, only to discover that alienation was just another form of pop culture. Holden Caulfield was every young rebel's hero. But I pined for home, for none of my American fellow students had the fire of my fellow Croats, smoking endless cigarettes and discussing the possibility of student government while they cynically appraised a girl as she walked on by. I saw Americans as shallow and conformist, brainwashed by pop culture; I did not understand that underneath the superficiality lay individuals capable of choosing their real lives—something we only talked about back home. The pop culture was just a part of that youthful exploration and experimentation that created options and opportunities. And then, in the sixties, all of America became the stage on which young Americans wore costumes and transformed themselves in public, making it clear that America was not only a "young" country but also the country of and for the young.

Then came Elvis Presley. But by then I was married to a man who scoffed at anything American. He had married me because I was "different" from anybody he knew and really removed from pop. He seduced me to the music of Bartok; we made love to Shostakovich. But my husband considered Jack Kerouac and Allan Ginsberg "highbrow" enough and we practiced being "beat," the only fashion our finances allowed us to pursue. I wore black tights and turtleneck shirts, and we rode bicycles all over Seattle. In the meantime, Elvis Presley rocked his fans unnoticed, but I avidly followed the Soviet Union's growing pains. Its poets became "pop"; Voznesensky and Evtushenko read their poems in soccer stadiums to huge crowds making even Khrushchev—relatively liberal—uneasy. By the time the Beatles came on the scene, I realized I had missed something. Besides, they were European, and I was a snob enough to think they had something to say, but the real reason was—still is—American pop culture overwhelmed me and frightened me. There is something raw in it, uncontainable; it seems to have no standards and it appeals to the adolescents in us as well as to the rebels. Only later did I realize how Elvis' gyrating pelvis liberated the Americans, who had been stilted and repressed in comparison to their more sophisticated European peers. The sexual revolution of the sixties was something we in Europe had gone through already. The women's movement, however, had a profound effect on me. I "found myself" and divorced my husband. Reinterpreting my mother's centuries-old dictum, "Women hold up three corners of the house," I did not wait for my next husband to court me. I courted him.

So I went to see the Beatles when they came to Seattle in 1963. I had never mixed with crowds as huge as those. My friends parked a mile away and we walked to the large stadium where the concert was held to the accompaniment of screaming girls and popping flashlights, which made it impossible to hear the music. Seattle in the sixties was a vast theatre: colorful hippies dotted the green lawns of the University of Washington campus; small theatres presented avant-garde plays; at the outskirts of Seattle, huge rock concerts took place, often compared to Woodstock. I heard Joan Baez there and saw my first topless girls. Even the snob of my soon-to-be-ex-husband decided "the scene" was rather interesting.

Later, my second husband, my children and I listened to the Beatles on

MELITA GARDNER

records. We bought records of other pop musicians, from Jefferson Airplane, to the Rolling Stones and Frank Zappa. I also listened to the music of protest, which I understood much better: Bob Dylan, Joan Baez. Our children were raised on pop music, Simon and Garfunkle and the Bee Gees among others; all our children love music and studied at least one instrument. One of our daughters was determined to become the first female rock musician in Pensacola (in the early 90's), so she organized a band. Ten years later she is still friends with several former members. Music bonds. My husband knew a lot about traditional and country songs and musicians and helped me understand the role of jazz and black musicians. I realized that the songwriters were really the poets of the people, the poets whose works ought to be taken seriously and anthologized. Apparently Dr. Millet of the English Department at the University of West Florida thought so too because, assisted by a graduate student, he edited and published a collection of rock musicians' lyrics.

What disturbed me most was the commercial exploitation of the pop stars. Graceland became a Mecca and spawned a few third-rate popular movies. The Beatles broke up and drifted into obscurity to be revisited on the anniversary of their appearance on the Ed Sullivan show. Pop culture influences our young enormously who consider it an initiation ritual to go to rock concerts, but few pop culture practitioners could have left such a mark on our culture as did the early rock musicians or movie stars. The more popular they became the less "real" they were. James Dean, Elvis Presley, Marilyn Monroe and John Lennon became "sublime" because they died young; Madonna and Michael Jackson have become ridiculous. Brittany Spears is on her way there.

The Croatian poet Vlado Gotovac, speaking of poems and songs (in Croatian, the word for both is the same), says:

> *A song is like a vessel with fire.*
> *It should be cool enough so we can carry it;*
> *it should be open so it can keep us warm.*
> *The intensity of fire we don't mention.*
> ("A Vessel with Fire," my translation)

Our singers tend to come too close to their own fire, which either burns them to death or disfigures them.

✶ ✶ ✶

THE GIRL WHO WAS AFRAID OF DOGS

Third Place Children's Fiction

Once there was as girl named Taylor. She was six years old. She had long dark straight hair, and she was thin. She had dark freckles under her dark mahogany brown eyes. She loved to play with her friends after school. She loved to jump rope, play board games such as Chutes and Ladders, Candy Land, and Operation, play hide and go seek, and follow the leader. Taylor loved to read; therefore, she went to the library down the street from her house to check out two to four books. She loved to read books about princes saving princesses or children her age getting into trouble. The only books she never checked out were books about dogs because she was afraid of them. She was afraid of small dogs, big dogs, and police dogs. She was afraid of every dog from Yorkshire Terriers to German Shepherds.

One day, Taylor heard a strange noise from under her father's rusty red truck. The noise sounded like whimpering. She did not know what it was, so she took a closer look. She saw a dog, and it was big and skinny. It had the head and face of a Golden Retriever. The eyes were bright emerald green. The dog's color looked like a German Shepherd's pattern of black and tan, and the tail looked like a Collie's with a feathering of white and brown. The dog just stared at Taylor, and it did not growl or bark. Taylor walked back a little - about two inches, and she was still looking at the dog. She was amazed it did not try to bite her. She was still frightened of the dog because it was so big. She went to the house and told her mom about the dog. Taylor's mom went outside to look at the dog, and she felt sympathy for the animal because it was stick thin. She went back into the house and filled an old bowl with water. The dog was gulping the water and panting afterwards. Taylor's mom asked her to come with her to the store to buy

NATASHA SANTO

dog food. At the store, Taylor's mom bought a can of moist dog food and a dog bowl. Taylor and her mom went home to feed the dog. Taylor's mom opened the can, placed the food in the bowl, and fed the dog outside. The dog did not seem afraid of Taylor's mom. Taylor watched the dog from the window. Taylor was shocked the dog did not try to bite her mother. She was fascinated by how the dog chewed its food and licked the bowl. Taylor's dad came home from work, and Taylor's mom told him about the dog and that she fed the dog and gave it water. Taylor's dad told her that once the dog was fed or given water it would never leave. He called the police about the dog, and the police said they would place an ad in the newspaper about a missing dog. The police said that after thirty days they could keep the dog or place it in the city pound.

While Taylor and her family waited for news about the dog, Taylor's mom kept feeding it and giving it water. Taylor watched from the window while her mom cared for the dog. After three days, she saw the dog did not bite her mother. The dog started to lick Taylor's mom's face and hand. She came to look at the dog, but she stayed about four inches away from the animal. After five days, she went about two inches closer to the dog. The whole time Taylor went towards the animal, the dog never bit, barked, or growled at Taylor. The next day, Taylor's mom asked her if she wanted to pet the dog. Taylor was slightly hesitant, so her mom took her hand toward the dog's head and moved her hand. Taylor was grateful the dog did not bite, bark, or growl at her, so her mom moved her hand slowly away from Taylor's. The dog licked Taylor's hand and face, and Taylor kept petting the animal. Afterwards, Taylor started to play catch by throwing tennis balls and sticks with the dog. Taylor also petted the dog's head and back and rubbed its belly. After thirty days, Taylor's dad called the police and asked about the dog. The police said no one claimed the animal, and the dog was his to keep. Taylor's dad asked if she wanted to keep the dog. Taylor said yes excitedly, and she named the dog Molly.

✳ ✳ ✳

That Palich Woman

Second Place Short Fiction

Long after I had gone to America, my friend Lydia wrote that Radovan's mother, Mrs. Palich, had died. Zagreb was my amputated limb, and every letter from home revived searing memories; Lydia's news touched on most. Even though I can't blame her for my decision to emigrate from Yugoslavia in 1956, she had played an important role in the defining events of the summer of 1951.

In 1950, I had turned sixteen and fallen in love with Radovan, his thin, pale face, black piercing eyes, even his round glasses, thin brown hair and blackheads on his foreheads. He and I wandered through the streets of Zagreb, lounged on the banks of the river Sava, ate chevapchichi, small skewered sausages, and when the first autumn rains came, took refuge among the tombs in spacious arcades of Mirogoy, the ancient Zagreb cemetery. We were old for our age, preoccupied with war, starvation and the atomic bomb. The dissolving faces of Japanese children stopped us from holding hands.

But next spring came the night when Radovan and I sat close, his arms around me, whispering our thoughts to each other. He pulled me closer, leaned over and kissed me suddenly, his lips taut with passion. His eyes were huge and dark with desire. Blood rushed into my cheeks, my hands shook, and my legs melted. I recovered only when I heard the tower strike midnight.

"Oh, late again," I jumped up and smoothed my skirt. "Mama won't let me see you."

I had to sit right down and press my hands on my wobbly knees. Closing my eyes, I took three deep breaths.

"Medieval customs," Radovan grumbled and pulled away. His head fell against the back of the bench. "As if we couldn't kiss any time."

I looked up at the full moon blanching the sky and sighed.

MELITA GARDNER

The kiss had made all the difference. We walked the streets of Zagreb intertwining our arms or stood in front of my door unable to say "good night."

A space opened before me and pulled me in, turbulent and vast, purging me of doubt and cynicism. All was forgotten but the face of the beloved; all was shrouded in mist except the caresses we constantly bestowed on each other. I saw only Radovan, my perfect lover.

And then she intervened, like the witch in Snow White. The Palich woman, Radovan's mother, steamed into our living room and sat down so hard Mama's heavy Habsburg chair groaned. Mama wasn't home; only my friend Lydia and I sat on the other side of the square dining room table that Mama insisted on covering with absurdly fine, lacy runners, which my fingers tended to unravel.

"If you don't leave my son alone, Veronica, I'll tell your mother I saw you with that old man," said Palichka, pulling herself up and tripling the double chin.

Two years earlier I had briefly dated an older man. Of course, she knew.

"It isn't any of your . . . " I began, but stopped short and clutched the runner. She really might tell Mama, and I would get an even stiffer curfew.

At my outburst, Palichka's cheeks paled and her hand fluttered to her large bosom. Her black eyes narrowed and the bushy eyebrows met. She got up, her thighs pushing the chair so it clattered to the floor. I ran around the table to help her, but she waved me off and reached for her cane. At the front door, she turned to me, raising the cane. I ducked.

"Don't worry. I wouldn't touch you."

I gasped and glanced at Lydia, still sitting at the table. She turned her head away, but her shoulders shook.

"I'll never cross this threshold again," said Palichka, glaring. "My poor heart . . ."

She did have a heart problem and was on medication. What if she died, here in Mama's parlor? And she wore black as if she were perpetually mourning somebody.

"Please stay, Mrs. Palich, I'll make a cup of strong coffee. To help your heart," I entreated.

A look stopped me from making an utter fool of myself. She let herself out of the apartment, but I followed her to the top of the stairs and waited until I heard the entrance door below crash. A peephole winked on my neighbor's door. Back in the apartment, Lydia was still laughing. My unhappy look persuaded her to clamp her lips tight.

"Don't worry," she soothed. "She won't die. She'll come back when she needs to borrow money from your mother. Her heart is just an excuse for not working. Look at your Mama. Takes in typing and substitutes in schools."

I sighed. "Papa was a communist, so Mama has connections. Palichka needs Mama. How do you think she has managed to keep that villa on Banska? Mama told Papa's old comrades in the government that Palichka had no source of income except her rental property. And the rent she charges is outrageous. Mama helped her keep an apartment all to herself, too. On account of her heart."

I didn't tell Mama about Palichka's visit but asked her what the woman had against me.

"Nothing," Mama reassured me. "She just doesn't want her precious Radovan supporting anybody except her. As an economist, he will make good money."

"Why does your mother hate me?" I asked Radovan after telling him about the visit.

He said nothing.

"Hey, Radovan, answer me," I boxed his arm.

He stopped walking. "How should I know? Every mother hates those that come between her and her child. Maybe all parents do. But think what mothers go through. They give birth to children in pain and raise them in pain and then somebody takes them away."

"My mother never talks about pain. But if your mother hates losing you so much, why doesn't she stop you from seeing me?"

He took me in his arms, but I never found out what Palichka really thought of me. In May, she came by to borrow money from Mama for a trip to Island Brach, one of the biggest and most beautiful islands in the Adriatic. Radovan would return the money after he collected the rents. Since the government had not confiscated land parcels under eight acres, Palichka was planning to sell her five acres on the island, cashing in on the renewed interest in tourism.

"You help him save some of the rent money," she told me at the door. I was too surprised to ask why she suddenly trusted me. All I could think about was that Palichka's whole apartment would be Radovan's, a luxury young people only dreamed about at the time when often two or three families shared an apartment.

I finished my junior year in high school, Radovan took his exams, and the summer heat set in. The villa on Banska stayed cool in the shade of the big chestnut tree in the yard. Plum trees shaded the steep path to the winding steps under the red brick roof. The yellow stucco walls made my fingers tingle when I brushed my hand across the surface; sweet-smelling acacia blooms covered the matching yellow garden wall, hiding the house from the street. Radovan and I spent afternoons drinking chilled raspberry juice and eating fried acacia blooms. We lay on the couch in the living room and kissed or danced rumba playing on the radio.

Then came the first of July and with it the rent money. After Radovan returned to Mama what he owed, he took me to sweet shops, restaurants, cafes. We sampled Napoleons, drank ice coffee, dined on chevapchichi.

The smell of fried pork sausage still reminds me of that summer. Streetcars took us to Maksimir Zoo where we fed the animals. On languid afternoons, Radovan rented a rowboat and pulled us along the shady side of the Maksimir Lake until the shadows reached the sunny side. When I told him I was supposed to watch his spending, he laughed.

But he did slow down. Instead of tickets to expensive events, he bought streetcar passes to the River Sava where we swam in the afternoon heat or took long walks on the green river banks, smelling of reeds and mud. On the way back, we jostled sweaty commuters going home from factories across the river.

We were desperately in love. Every time we looked at each other, we had to kiss; we touched as though we needed to make sure the other one was still there; we breathed in each other's smell. And suddenly, sex and love were in the air. It seemed that everybody around us was kissing, and our friends were full of stories of who had done it with whom. I discussed sex even with my priest in the confessional and came to the conclusion it could not be a sin if you loved somebody as I loved Radovan. Our love, our moment-by-moment pleasure in each other, the sense of freedom and release it offered us precluded thoughts about the future, dark and forbidding.

And so we decided it was time we consummated our love, but when I arrived at his apartment on the appointed day, Radovan couldn't go through with "violating me." He felt the act would kill or desecrate our love. Instead, he took me for dinner in the restaurant on Tsmrok where I downed glass after glass of wine, a desperate heroine's gesture. Afterwards, Radovan pulled me down on a bench in the park nearby and kissed me until I ached, but I had no energy to resist even though I knew what Mama would say. In the midnight-dark sky, stars blazed brighter than ever.

"My god, where have you been?" Mama grabbed my arm when I stumbled in at two in the morning.

"Don't worry, Mama, I'm okay," I laughed.

"You're not going anywhere for three days," she said sternly. "You and Radovan are spending too much time together. And drinking up all the rent money. Shame on you."

I agreed with Mama. It occurred to me that Radovan was tired of me. Men needed each other to do men-things together.

"Tell him I'm not home when he comes," I told Mama and collapsed on my bed.

I spent the next three days cleaning the house: washing the windows, all double, scrubbing the floors, beating the dust out of rugs. And listening to music. The man in the apartment above us was a pianist and played for hours, mostly Chopin, who took my breath away and made me cry.

The third day Lydia came by and, surprised to find me at home, suggested we go for a stroll on the Corso where young people walked and flirted with each other, but when I shook my head, she looked at me hard and gave me a piece of worldly wisdom.

"Little girl, you're lovesick. Struck by the gods. We'll have to do something about it."

She stayed with me all evening, telling me the latest gossip. I found out little, snub-nosed Mira had a serious boyfriend. Marian and Senda went on vacation together. Beba, the class beauty, gave a dinner party to celebrate the loss of her virginity. In the middle of the dinner, she toasted her friends, put on a jazz record and took her boyfriend to her bedroom. After a while, she rejoined them. The story made me feel really out of touch, so I told Lydia about Radovan and me.

"His mother," Lydia concluded immediately. "She has cowed him so much he can't make love to a girl. Pretty sad, really."

I nodded. Lydia's diagnosis sounded right, so I asked, "What now?"

Lydia had an instant reply. "A Platonic love affair. Any girl would envy you. Most guys want to get into his girl's pants right away. I know."

The next day I went to Radovan's house to see if Lydia was right, but Radovan and I avoided the subject. We put on bright smiles and went walking on Tsmrok. We were uncomfortable, both of us talking too much. Only when we got to our little park on top of the hill, deserted on a week night, did he relax and, whistling "Maritsa," put his arm around my shoulders. When we got up, he pecked my cheek.

Soon Radovan was his old, carefree self. He came by and, waving a record in front of me, suggested we go to his place. "Lotte Lenya. You can't get her records around here."

"Where did you find it?"

"Our tenant has an uncle in Germany."

Lotte Lenya's strident voice and the harsh message of her songs suited us perfectly. Much later, in America, did I realize why she and "Mack the Knife" were so popular. It was not so much the capitalistic system Kurt Weil's music rejected as human callousness and greed that I had come to consider the cause of all human suffering. If Radovan and I could be true to each other and value each other above anything else, we could be saved.

But that day I also discovered he connected Kurt Weil with something else: suicide, self-destruction. For him, there was no salvation, no way out. Oh, he kissed me and fondled me. For a brief moment I thought he had overcome his qualms when, in the grip of passion, he took off my underpants.

He shook his head, "It's still no good, Veronica. But we don't need to suffer."

He got up and soon returned. Holding hands we walked out into the fresh evening air and the sound of birds roosting for the night. Radovan reached into his pocket and took out a small vial.

He whispered, "Let me see if there's enough for both of us."

The small brown bottle said "Belladonna." Radovan opened it and peered in. He smelled the contents and juggled the vial. In the gathering gloom, I could see it was a quarter full; I could see his mother's name on it and the instructions to take a spoonful for heart palpitations. Radovan capped the vial and shook his head.

"Barely enough to give us nightmares."

"How do you know?" I demanded, the idea of dying together suddenly the logical solution.

"I tried it," he made a face. "At first it is great, visions, images, euphoria. I didn't take quite enough to kill me, I discovered, but enough to scare the shit out of me."

And the vial went flying into the neighbor's thick lilac bushes. Radovan thrust his hands into his pockets and, whistling the Marseillaise, walked down the hill toward Ilitsa.

"Come on, race you to the Republic Square," he shouted as he broke into a run. Beads of sweat slid down his forehead when he stopped, but his eyes were still bloodshot.

"Let me take you home," he finally said.

I clung to him and tried to change his mind. What if he goes back and drinks the vial? It wouldn't be too hard to find it among the bushes. But he just took my hands, smiled and stroked my cheek. Then, guessing my thoughts, he let my hands drop. "Don't worry, I won't drink it. I'm a coward."

I didn't visit the villa again. He went on another spending spree, which I refused to join, so we didn't see each other for a while. I didn't tell anybody about our aborted suicide attempt, not even to Lydia.

One day, Radovan came by and handed me a blue velvet box.

"Open," he ordered.

In the box lay a long strand of small, irregular pearls, each of a different sheen.

"Where did you get these?" I asked, holding them at arm's length.

"Somebody needed money," was all he said.

"I can't take them."

He closed my hand over the box. "You must. A token of our perfect love."

At the end of August, Palichka returned from her island. The day after her arrival she exploded through the front door of our apartment without a "hello." She sank into a chair and glared at me and at Mama.

"What is it?" asked Mama.

"What did that slut of yours do to my son?" she leaned toward Mama. Mama sat up straight and waited for the woman to continue.

"My son spent all the rent money for two months. On her."

"Are you sure he spent it on me?" I asked.

She dismissed my question with a gesture and began a lecture. "Bad blood always shows. I told Radovan to leave trash alone. Your father was kicked out of college, lost every job he had, lived off your mother's inheritance. How could he possibly teach you the value of money?"

The logic of the argument escaped me but not the insult. I opened my mouth to say something, but she went on.

"That man abandoned everything, all his responsibilities, just to run around with rebels and ne'er do wells, desecrating his family crest."

I jumped up and confronted her, hands on hips fishwife style. "At least he fought for his principles. You live off other people, your tenants, your son. My poor Radovan. What have you done to him?"

In a terrible voice, she demanded I apologize; Mama and I just saw her to the door.

After that scene, Mama decided I couldn't see Radovan. That meant we had to hide in lovers' lanes in Tushkanac or walk to the end of Tsmrok. The fall rains set in, so we started meeting on Mirogoy again. When the weather was nice we sat on a bench near the entrance, watched the rose colored walls glow in the sunset and talked; when it rained we walked inside arcades housing important family vaults lit by perpetual candles.

One day he took me to a large arcade under a small turret with a window. Across from the tomb burned a candle next to a small bench. I read the plaque on the tomb, Milan Palich, 1895-1946.

"Your father?" I asked. He nodded and sat on the bench with an expression I couldn't read. After a long silence, he sighed.

"Damn bastard. I can still remember the scenes when he came home late. Usually drunk."

And Radovan told me things he had probably told nobody else about the times he spent hiding under the dining room table, listening to his father's whine and his mother's rage.

"She used to wait for him with the rolling pin. Sometimes she hit him. Then he would spend even more time away. I didn't know whether to hate him or her."

I could see him as a small child, terrified, and I thanked God that my father had died before I could witness such scenes.

"You're lucky your father is dead," Radovan echoed my thought.

Years passed. Radovan married a nurse and had a beautiful daughter. Lydia, who knew his wife, told me Palichka treated the woman like a servant. I was finishing my studies in English and German. It turned out I

MELITA GARDNER

had a gift for languages, a very useful gift in those days when all young people yearned to escape the narrow confines of the communist Yugoslavia. Few were given the opportunities or the means of escape. I would get away, but first had to suffer the greatest grief of all, my mother's death of a heart attack.

Mama's body was taken to the mortuary on Mirogoy, where it lay in the Little Chapel, surrounded by flowers. She had many friends, as did I, and they all brought chrysanthemums.

Outside, rain wept and turned to sleet in the cold February mist. We stood around the coffin, praying, when a woman fell onto the coffin of her child next to my mother's coffin and keened, emitting the most heart-wrenching sound I had ever heard. I shook all over and collapsed on a bench outside, crying into my scratchy shawl.

When the heaves subsided, from the corner of an eye I saw Palichka. She was coming toward me, hands outstretched. I took a deep breath, looked her in the eyes, and shook her hand, thanking her for coming. For Mama's sake.

And now the woman was dead. As I read Lydia's letter, I recalled my last meeting with Radovan: the soft evening air, the glow in the west, the balmy wind. Before I left for America, I had taken the pearls to him in his office. "For your daughter. So she can get away from your mother."

He said nothing, but his look spoke of longing and resignation. I almost told him to run away with me.

The Palich woman, Lydia wrote, had died of old age. Nothing much was wrong with her. Lydia's letter fell on my desk, covering my students' papers, and I wept as I had not wept since my mother's funeral; I wept for the love I still bore Radovan, so pure, so brittle. It had lodged in my heart like a grain of sand, and time had rubbed it to a shiny pearl.

✶ ✶ ✶

Fear's Birth

First Place Poetry

A wake of exhaust fumes and black smoke
lingered long after the National Guard tanks
rumbled by our house,
its stench so similar to the marchers' torches the night before.
I wondered if Mother
would lock us in the bathroom again,
if our pillows
would be hardened by the porcelain tub,
our shoulders
stiffened by the tile wall and floor.
I wondered if our dreams
would always be tormented by dark figures,
our angry friends,
seeking justice for the senseless death of their leader,
the good Reverend King.
I wondered if fear
tastes like the mildewed shower curtain I
clinched between my teeth
as the fathers of my schoolmates
broke every window on the front of our house.

JACQUELINE BOUCHARD

Justice Brings Me No Solace

First Place Short Fiction

"*W*hy do you keep calling him my stepfather? He's my mother's husband. He never adopted me." She has all the confidence of a woman who has, for the first time, been told she is beautiful, has just discovered the joy of believing it, and now intends her faith in herself to be a proud tribute to the man who first recognized her for who she wants to be.

My boss always acts as if my smile is the smile of the young girls who ignored him in high school, their regard, through me, finally bestowed upon him, something they did not know well enough to give.
He pretends to see this with the eyes that do not deign to wander down to my blouse or my legs but nonetheless are fixated there. He would never be so crass or so obvious: He restricts himself to comments on my clothes, on their color or print, never the style. He has practiced law nearly as long as I have been alive, so the threat he poses for me is much more clear, much less overtly physical. And always he gives me a genuine smile, as if it is a secret between us, that I choose my clothes just for him.
He is a thin old man with fair skin and liver spots, pale brown eyes and thinning hair, of median height, the sort of man who is invisible even in a room crowded by things and not people. In a courtroom, juries are typically indifferent to him, sometimes put-off, less-often warm. He may remind them of the neighbor who never bothers them, a kindly uncle, or a cruel father.

She is a wide-hipped college freshman now, her pants worn tight and low-waisted. While I am out of the office to make a fresh copy of her statement, she leans over my desk to read from my file, and when I return I see a slash of unblemished white skin stretching above her nylon underwear, her thin white cotton shirt too short, pulled tight across her back.
When I enter she sits up slowly, as if to say, "Because I can," but she does not look at me.

"Are you ready?" My boss asks.

No. "Yes," I say. I am as ready as any other attorney would expect me to be. I have read the reports. I have seen the videos. I have made a list of the questions that should be answered. But I do not feel ready to face either girl—Child M or Child C, as their names will be written in the transcript made after trial. M, raped by her father for three years, beginning when she was six and ending when she was nine. C, raped by her father when she was still younger.

"We'll do it in my office," my boss says, turning to go out of mine.

So I take my yellow pad of paper, my list of questions typed out on the computer, and I carry these to the lobby, to see, there, slouched uncomfortably with eyes on the floor, C and M, and their mother.

I met their mother to arrange for this interview. She is a hard-faced woman, perhaps five years my senior but much older. Her hair is black, wavy and long, colored auburn some time ago, the dye now five inches from her roots, covering her ears and the sides of her face, as if she would choose to hide behind it. Her bangs are low over her brows, into her brown eyes, and she has a tendency to lift her head and shake it a little, to move a few of these strands away from her eyes, but temporarily. Her mouth is lined with the beginning of smoker's wrinkles and as my eyes settle on them I think of the notes in the girls' medical records, the providers recording their attempts to get both parents to stop smoking to ease their daughters' asthma.

She is the sort of woman who seems to live perpetually in the same five-year-old T-shirt, long faded to thin yellow, and baggy jeans wearing thin across the seat.

She looks at me as she has looked at me before, into my eyes but without directness, without challenge.

I smile with my lips and she does the same. I turn to the girls and introduce myself but neither of them meets my gaze. C smiles and giggles even as M slumps in her chair. I know they are as I have seen them portrayed in their doctor's reports, in their teacher's evaluations, and even in the video they did with Child Protective Services. C, now nine, is at once more and less likeable than her sister.

C sits upright, leans toward me, eager, her eyes wide. She says hello and giggles again. She has two small toys in her hands, one a little pony and the other a doll, almost the same size. She holds them out to me. "See?" She says, and the hand with the doll places it atop the pony.

M sits slumped in her chair, eyes averted, quiet, she does not move, does not try, even, to mumble a hello, as her sister did.

"Yes, you have a beautiful pony there. Ponies are great," I smile and say. After a pause I continue, extending my hand toward M, "We'd like to talk to [M] first, if you don't mind." I say it to both M and her mother.

JACQUELINE BOUCHARD

M nods without lifting her head to me, rising slowly from the chair as if she were an old woman who needed to use her arms as much as her legs.

I hear my own words in my head. "If you don't mind." Of course she minds. The mother and the daughter. The mother has said many times she wants only to have her family back together.

The psychologist tells us M is only vaguely aware of the harm her father has caused, and C is not aware of it at all, that in her many fights with her sister she blames the older girl for their separation from their father. We know that the investigators have told their mother that if she allows the fighting to continue, or if she herself in any way suggests that M is at fault, both C and M will be taken from her, and this is the only reason she cooperates.

My boss would say what I could not, that we have this in common with her, our concern for the girls.

M and I walk down the hall together in silence, because I do not want to lead the way, and I try to think of something comforting to say, as I always do, and I always fail, knowing that I cannot imagine what all this means to them.

We enter my boss' office, warm with leather and plush rugs, soft, sand-colored walls, and wood-framed prints of the beach. He rises with a smile, coming from behind his desk with his hand extended. M takes it with an averted face, a small grin on her lips, as if this were an embarrassing, grown-up thing.

He gestures toward one of the big leather chairs and she takes it, sinking down into it as she had sunk into the front lobby chairs, her eyes this time on her sneakered feet. It is perhaps one hundred degrees outside but, like her mother, she wears jeans. M's T-shirt is newer, though, white cotton, still fresh, an embroidered line of flowers along the collar.

My boss and I sit across from her, our backs to his desk.

He starts out by telling her about his own children, the youngest of whom, he claims, to be nearly M's age. She has, in fact, graduated from high school, but I sit quiet.

He comes to the questions as I have seen him do before, by asking where she has lived and how old she was, what school she went to and who were her friends, and although these are intended to be the easy questions, she answers with her forehead turned to the floor, her eyes averted. After she recites the address of the home where she lived when she was six years old, he asks her about penises and vaginas, about the words she uses for them, about the word she used for the dildo her father had her insert in his anus. As she answers these questions she puts her hands to her forehead and pauses a long time, as if dragging the answers out from someplace far away. She answers without emotion, yet as if every word is more than three syllables in a new and difficult language.

She says nothing we did not know and she repeats everything consistently, down to the things she does not remember. In this she is different from the many other victims we see, who seem to recall more with each repetition.

He asks other questions that were not clear from the investigation or the videotape. "Did your father ever get angry at you over this? Did he offer you gifts for not telling?" These are standard questions: This behavior is common with child molesters. "Is it wrong for fathers to have sex with their daughters?"

At this I look at him as if I am facing the anger this new question provokes in me.

"Yes." For her this is nearly an immediate response.

"Why?"

She shifts her weight in the chair and it squeaks back at her.

Eventually, she answers, "Because it would be wrong for the girl to get pregnant."

I look at my boss to see if he is pleased with this answer. I do not know what passes under his now-unreadable face. He is not unkind, really, not hard, but just the same I want to stand and thank her, to take her from this room, yet I know he would stop me.

Instead he has a few closing comments, explaining to her the process, that we will likely need her to testify, that we will contact her through her mother, that later we will prepare her for cross-examination. He asks if she has any questions, anything more to tell him, and she asks about her sister, if we will need her, too.

"Yes," he answers.

It is lucky for us that each daughter had come upon her father, at least once, having sex with her sister.

I stand in front of the jury and force myself to be the woman I want them to see.

In the name of all those victims who did cry out, who did fight, they want to know why she didn't cry out and fight back as a rape victim should. She told them why but she couldn't explain it to them. I could see the doubt in their eyes, as I saw it in my boss' eyes, when he told me that if I wanted to take this case I would have to do it alone, and I knew it was because he wanted to continue to be able to say he had not lost a case in 20 years.

A psychologist tried to explain it, too. But they need more than to hear it is not unusual for a victim to act as she did. That does not explain *why*. It only tells them that it happens. And I chose not to allow the psychologist

JACQUELINE BOUCHARD

to tell them she was sexually abused as a child, I chose not to allow this to the defense.

I cannot testify, I cannot tell them what my experience has taught me. I am sure he chose her carefully, he sought her out for those residual effects — those things they saw on the witness stand but could not recognize — her easily averted eyes, her uncertainty, the way, even under the defense counsel's cross examination, she shows a desire to please. She cannot trust her own instincts.

This he must have sensed when he maneuvered himself closer to her at the bar, listening for the easy, nervous giggle she would give in response to her friends, watching for the eyes she refused to lift to search her surroundings. He waited until she ventured to say something and then he broke into the conversation, easily and with self-assurance, confirming that she allowed him to interrupt and guide the discussion, never returning to her topic.

He ensured that when he slipped his arm around her waist and leaned in to whisper in her ear, she did not give in to the cringe he saw in her shoulders or to the furtive glance that went, just once, to her friends, as they drew into closer conversation with one another.

It would be only when they were alone that she would turn her face from his kisses, but even then she wouldn't run. And when he would grab her cheeks forcefully to turn them toward his lips, she wouldn't pull away, she would only roll her eyes downward.

On the witness stand, prompted by my questions, she told the jury some of this, slouching to hide her breasts inside her elbows in a way that made me fear for her. Juries want to find the truth bold and self-righteous.

When she told them he threw her on the bed I know they did not understand, they thought that perhaps she laid there, waiting for him, when she should have screamed. She could not explain that there was no space between their two bodies, it had been his weight as much as his hands that pushed her backward, his body following the force of his own arms so that he landed on top of her even as she landed on the bed, and immediately he began to fumble with her clothes.

She said she tried to fight him off, telling him "No," and then, finally, turning her head against the mouth that was now mumbling profanities, as she pushed his hands away with her own. But he ignored her. It was only later that she realized her resistance then had helped him, forced her hips up against him and lifted her weight from the bed.

She told the jury she knew her upper body was weak so she concentrated on her legs and when he lifted above her to unbutton his own jeans she got in a good kick. She told them he paused for a second and so did she. He grimaced and she thought for a moment it was over, he would get up and leave her. She distinctly remembered saying his name at this point and telling him to stop.

But he did not stop. Instead he began again with greater fury, his fingers grasping her arms tight enough to leave bruises, his knees forcing her thighs apart.

And so she froze.

I had told her in her interview that the defense attorney would use this against her. She could try to explain it, I said, to diffuse it during her direct examination.

But she had not been able to explain it, then, during the interview, nor could she explain it at the trial. Instead she cried. And, as the defense counsel continued to berate her, she could only say she didn't know why she didn't act as they all thought she should have.

And now I must make the men see they are not at the defense table: She is not the girl whose head they pushed in high school. I must make the women see that they should not disown her, that claiming her does not make all of us more vulnerable.

They give him a year in jail. The attorneys in the office know this is a compromise verdict; the jury found him guilty by a bare majority, and those who believed him guilty were able to persuade the undecided by a promise of a light sentence. He will be out in perhaps ten months, with good behavior.

The victim is there to hear the sentence, and I hear her choke a cry when the foreman speaks. I look back at her after the judge closes the court, unsure whether I should apologize or console. So instead I stand beside her and extend my hand to touch her arm, slowly. She nods and wipes the tears away but they keep coming.

After a pause I mumble, "If you need anything…"

Her mother has sat through the entire trial, and now she looks at me with hard, unforgiving eyes.

It is not something to celebrate, but I do. I go out with my two good friends and my best friend's longtime boyfriend, my other friend's latest date.

After a few hours the two men go to a sports bar next door, but we stay to dance a little longer. When we leave we move in single file toward the front entrance, past the bar, and suddenly my arm is grabbed, tightly, from behind, and immediately, instinctively, I shake it off with the forward momentum of my step. I glance back to see only a mustached, blond face, red drunken eyes, a silver earring.

For a moment I am shamed by my own intoxication, by my own sudden awareness that I had failed, for the past hour, to know my surround-

JACQUELINE BOUCHARD

ings, to scan for men such as this, to know those who are looking for prey.

Still, I am gone through the crowd, my eyes on the backs of my unseeing friends. I want to reach them, to warn them, because I do not know if he will follow us, or if, like those three men last year who formed the gauntlet for us at that other bar, this minor assault is enough.

When I get home that night I look in the mirror at my face and I wonder what it is in it that made the man grab me. I am not looking for beauty. I am too experienced to believe, as the untouched women may, that only the pretty ones are harassed. For all their insecurity and accustomed invisibility, the plain ones are attractive targets as well.

If I do not push her I will certainly lose the case. She will lie or refuse to testify. She was only thirteen, then. Now, at eighteen, she maintains she still loves her stepfather. She feels responsible for their relationship, and not in the way M might later feel responsible but in the way a grown woman claims her first romance — it did not happen to be: she caused it, enjoyed it, cherished each moment so that she could remind herself that she was once worthy of a great love. And now we would take this from her.

Her mother is pressuring her to ignore the subpoena.

"Look," I say. She must see this is not, simply, a family matter but a criminal one as well. "Look, there were only two ways for this relationship with your stepfather to have ended, right?" *She cringes at the word "stepfather." Still she will not give me even this. Her eyes search the floor, but fiercely, as if in doing so she can gather ammunition to use against me.*

"You could have married him, right?"

At this she clicks her tongue and her eyes flit across mine. I see her as she must have been five years ago, her vulnerability thinly masked as contempt.

"Or you would break up with him."

She does not give me this, either.

"If, as you tried to do, you break off the relationship, he will continue to use his power as stepfather over you. That is what he is doing here." *I tap a finger over a copy of the letters he wrote to her during her freshman year at college. He called her a whore and a bitch, he threatened to abandon her to the multiple male acquaintances he accused her of sleeping with, to convince her mother she is a dirty slut, to prohibit her siblings from seeing her.* "This is not a power most lovers have over one another."

She says nothing but I continue. "If you were to marry him, these two children you've been calling your brother and your sister — "*and I know I have her here. Even though she has not lifted her eyes to me, her body has gone rigid. I know she loves her siblings. These are the innocents, the six-year-old son and ten-year-old daughter of her mother and stepfather. She desperately wants me to denigrate them in some way, to become the evil she can attack with justification and self-*

righteousness, in the name of love. "They would be calling you stepmother, and your child would be both their half-sibling and their niece or nephew," I add.

She stands, suddenly, in front of me, her hands clinched at her sides, and I know for a brief instant, before leaving, she considers hitting me.

✶ ✶ ✶

AUDREY WENDLAND

On Belay With Johnny

Second Place Non-Fiction

When I joined the Tenth Mountain Infantry in the summer of 1943, I never expected to get a bunkmate like Johnny Dolan. He was a tall, gangly Irish kid from New Jersey, cocky and sure he could handle anything rugged training at Camp Hale could dish out. We were both just out of high school and didn't know the half of it. The camp sat on top of the Continental Divide in Colorado, at an altitude so high and with air so thin you could hardly breathe. It took a couple of weeks to get "acclimatized" enough to even begin basic.

Right from the start, Johnny and I engaged in a kind of friendly rivalry. We both were entranced with the idea of actually being in the ski troops, the most elite outfit in the army, but it was hard to compete with Johnny. I stood only five foot seven and topped the scales at 120. He outweighed me by forty pounds. I was a city kid and not an outdoorsman like most of the other recruits. I never had even been hunting. But I had taken up weight lifting at a gym so I was wiry and strong. Johnny had superb coordination and only his eyesight kept him from becoming an expert at every sport. He wore thick, steel-rimmed glasses that fogged up and almost drove him nuts. Johnny hated those glasses. So I had him on that point. I had 20/20 vision and could easily outscore him on the rifle range.

Johnny had a deadpan sort of wry humor and I liked the way he'd never give up. If I'd be better at one stage of the training, he'd outperform me on another. I knew that once we got out on the slopes, he'd beat me all hollow. Johnny had been skiing since he was eight and I never had been on skis in my life. That was how the summer went. He'd rib me about my less-than-athletic build, and I'd give him a hard time about wearing those God-awful, army-issued glasses. Then we were assigned to the same squad after basic was over, and the competition became even more intense. We were learning reconnaissance, and I was blessed with a keen sense of direction. I had no trouble finding my way back to the starting point, even at midnight.

"Jeeze!" Johnny would say when the scores were posted. That was his favorite expression of dismay. Then he'd debate about how my route was easier than his and remind me that he always got the better-looking girls when we went on a weekend pass. We became inseparable, almost like brothers, although I had the feeling he didn't quite accept me as an equal. He just had to maintain his superior edge.

Summer faded into the glorious autumn you get in the Rockies and at last, we were ready to begin climbing mountains. Johnny was going to be my partner and I could hardly wait. This would be my chance to prove I was just as good as he was, if not better.

We were issued knee-length khaki shorts and lightweight shirts, plus combat helmets and mountain boots. The squad marched out to Homestead Creek to set up a tent village at the base of the tallest mountain I'd ever seen. For the next few weeks, under the supervision of instructors, we learned how to tie every kind of knot known to man; we scrambled over rocky slopes, up narrow chimneys, and rappelled down fifty-foot drops from the cliffs. We learned how to drive pitons into minute cracks in the rock, and how to listen for the ascending scale of ringing "clangs" that told us these metal foothold spikes had been hammered in securely.

Then we started the actual climbing, roped into teams of two or three. We rigged and rode aerial tramways suspended from the rocks above, and scaled impossible routes with one foot in a sling on a dangling rope. We learned the theory and practice of belay, a system designed to prevent a deadly fall. Basically, two men are tied together at the waist with a 120-foot length of nylon rope. If one team member should fall, the other one could limit the length of the fall by looping a piece of the rope around his waist and assuming a protective stance. I knew the procedure by heart.

The day of the big test dawned bright and clear. This was a sort of final exam in mountain climbing, our last chance to show our stuff and get rated on our skills. So it came as no surprise when Johnny announced he wanted to be the leader of our team. "Hope you don't mind," he added.

"It's okay," I replied. I had expected that. Even after all this practice, Johnny still didn't have much confidence in me as an athlete. The instructors spread out the squad in two-man teams, to begin the climb up a cliff pocketed with sharp overhangs. We scrambled upward with Johnny leading the way, searching for just the right spot to begin the belay part of the climb. He paused on a narrow granite ledge about two hundred feet above the valley floor.

"You're sure this is a good place?" I asked.

"As good as any," he replied. "See that nice stump of pine tree? Looks like a perfect mooring spot. You sit there and I'll tell you when I'm ready."

For the next part of the test, Johnny was supposed to continue climbing up the cliff for about thirty feet or so, while I waited below to act as the anchor. At that height, if he should slip, the most he could fall would be only sixty feet. I felt I could handle that. I sat on the ledge, straddled the 12-inch stump, and prepared my safety loop. I ran my end of the rope through my right hand, across my lower back and through my left hand. I dropped the loop of one hundred feet of rope over the ledge and secured it to a knot around my waist. I double-checked to be sure all the knots were tight. According to the principal of belay, the friction of the rope would act as a brake, if my partner should fall. Feeling all set, I glanced straight down from the ledge. It looked awfully far to the bottom of that valley.

"On belay!" Johnny shouted through cupped hands and I could hear the echo resound against the canyon walls. That was the signal he was ready to start climbing.

"On belay!" I hollered back.

Then Johnny took another hard look downward and his jaw tightened. "Jeeze!" he said. He took off his glasses and cleaned them with a bit of spit and his handkerchief. He squinted at me from behind the steel-framed spectacles. He adjusted his helmet and drew a deep breath.

"Climbing," he announced and started up the face of the rock. His fingers searched for narrow cracks to grab hold. His toes hunted for nubs wide enough to support the slender edge of his boot. We had been taught to move only one limb at a time—first a hand and then a foot. Cautiously, Johnny crept upward. I craned my neck to watch his slow progress and then he stopped moving. He just hung there, spread-eagled against the rock about thirty feet above me. I felt a sudden tingle of alarm. The rope between us still had enough slack for him to move around but I didn't like the look of his position. A huge overhang jutted out only a few feet above his head.

"Back off," I yelled. "That overhang is too big. You can't climb over it."

"I can't see my feet," he yelled back. "I'll have to try."

Gingerly, he crept upward until his fingers reached the top of the overhang. He hung onto it, while the toe of his boot kept searching and searching in vain for some new crevice. Then his left foot slipped and he started to slide. The friction of his body held him tight against the rock—but he was sliding, sliding, down, down, down toward the canyon floor.

Adrenaline shot through me. I dug my heels into the rock. I held the downhill section of the rope against my waist. I needed to let it out slowly, to provide enough friction for the brake when Johnny's 160-pound weight would reach the end of the tether. Otherwise, the force of the pull could yank me right off the stump. I was in a cold sweat. Then suddenly, my mind went blank. I couldn't remember which hand held the "downhill" section of the rope. Right or left? With no time to puzzle that out, I wrapped both hands around my waist and pressed my legs against the stump. I braced myself. Seconds later, the full force of Johnny's weight spun me around like a top. I found myself hanging upside down, my head against the rock and my eyes staring at the blue sky above. I was completely disoriented and too dazed to realize I had let Johnny fall the entire 120-foot length of the rope.

My hands still held on, my legs were still wrapped around the stump, but every muscle in my body was screaming in agony. Down below, I could see Johnny dangling from the rope, his body swinging in gentle arcs like a giant pendulum.

"Johnny!" I yelled. "Are you okay?"

Silence. No answer. The pain was excruciating. The weight was about to pull the rope right out of my hands and me with it. My legs could give out at any moment. "Medic!" I screamed.

"Hang on! We're coming!" I heard a chorus of yells and saw some of my fellow troopers climbing up in my direction. Beads of sweat rolled into my eyes. Fatigue tore at my muscles. Just when I thought I couldn't hang on for one more moment, I felt the rope go slack. Someone down below had lifted off the weight, leaving me light-headed and dizzy with relief. Now an instructor stood over me and grabbed me by the shirt. He hauled me upright and expertly wrapped the rope around his own shoulder. "On belay!" he shouted.

"Climbing," came the answer. It was Johnny's voice.

A few minutes later, Johnny's head appeared above the ledge. His face looked naked without the steel-rimmed glasses and his helmet was gone. Another instructor boosted him over the ledge and explained how he had reached a dazed and almost unconscious Johnny, and had pulled him into the shelter of a narrow cleft. A couple of minutes later, the instructor had ordered Johnny back up the ridge. These instructors believed in the philosophy of horsemanship. If you get thrown, you get right back into the saddle.

* * * * *

An hour later, in complete silence, Johnny and I shuffled along the trail that led back to our mountain tents. We had gone over every detail of the accident with the instructors—the forbidding overhang in the cliff, the slipped foot, my confusion about which hand held the downhill section of the rope. Everything. I almost had killed us both.

Now we had nothing more to say. We walked with heads hanging down, with a tumult of thoughts unspoken. I was sure Johnny could never forgive me for being such an idiot. Suddenly, he stopped in mid-path to squint at me with his near-sighted eyes, with that deadpan expression on his face I knew so well. Then he threw his arm around my shoulders and his somber face broke into a grin.

"Jeeze! You ass-hole," he said. "You made me break my goddam glasses."

That was how I knew everything between us was all right again, and that Johnny Dolan and I would be friends forever.

Friend

Honorable Mention Poetry

like wet snow clinging

        to an evergreen tree

I seek you out

        during the storm

today

        the bough weighs heavy

            with need

# Tigra's Quest

First Place Children's Fiction

With her belly full of warm milk, Tigra released a soft contented purr and stretched her small brown and black body to full length. She raised a white paw to her mouth and began her after dinner bath.

The barn door creaked open admitting a stream of moonlight into the darkness revealing her family snuggled at the base of a haystack. Must be that old farmer trying to run her family off again, Tigra thought. Why does he always come at bath time?

She nestled closer to her mama and four brothers and watched the farmer with half shut eyes. Suddenly, a large hairy hand scooped up her mama and two of her brothers, dropping them into a burlap sack.

"Tigra … Kit Kat … Tommy. Run … hide," her mama meowed from the bag.

Tigra burrowed deep into the hay, but still heard the muffled voice of the farmer. "The last thing I need around here are more cats," he said. "You can hide, but I'll get you sooner or later."

The barn door slammed shut. A frightened Tigra remained hidden deep in the haystack. What did he mean he'd get them all, she wondered, and where had he taken her mama and brothers?

Moments later when things were quiet, she crawled from her hiding place and called out. "Kit Kat? … Tommy? Are you here?" They didn't answer. "Okay, you two quit playing games. We've got to find mama and the others." Still no answer.

"He got them, too," a deep voice hooted from above. "If I were you, I'd get as far away from here as you can."

"Where did he take them?" Tigra gazed up at the rafters, her eyes wide with alarm.

"Don't know," said the owl. "But it can't be good."

"How do I get out of here," she asked.

"There's a knothole next to the barn door. You can squeeze through and make your get away."

Tigra scampered to the hole and yelled up. "Thanks," she said, and then wiggled through the opening.

"Ha! I knew you'd try to escape through here," the farmer said. He grabbed Tigra by the scruff of the neck.

She wiggled and squirmed, but he held tight. As he dropped Tigra into a sack, she saw owl flap his massive wings and fly into the night.

"Sorry, kid," he said. "But didn't want you cats eating up my winter supply of mice. There isn't enough to share."

Moments later, Tigra hurled through space, tumbled head over heels, and then landed with a thump.

Where am I, she wondered? She steadied her legs and tried to stand. The truck jerked forward and tossed her on her back. "Mama? ... Tommy? ... Kit Kat? Are you here?" All she heard was the rumble of the truck's engine. She called again. "Sandy? ... Rocky?" Still no answer.

Tigra sighed. "Guess no one's here but me," she sniffed. A tear trickled down her nose. She wiped it away and narrowed her eyes. Mama wouldn't like it if she saw me now, she thought. She taught me to be strong and brave.

The truck engine stopped and the cab door slammed. Tigra tried to stand again, but was swallowed deep within the folds of the burlap sack. Footsteps crunched in the gravel and came closer.

"No you don't, Mr. Farmer, not without a fight," she meowed, and then struggled to get up. Now on her feet she humped her back and extended her claws.

The farmer grabbed the bag from the truck, held it away from his body and laughed. "You just thought you'd get a swipe at me, little tiger. Well, I'm smarter than you."

She squirmed and clawed at the bag, but the farmer only laughed louder. "You're a lively one, but not for long," he said, and then pitched the bag as far as he could throw.

Tigra flew through the air and landed with a splash. Water rushed into the sack. She choked and sputtered, fighting to catch her breath. She kicked and meowed, but the bag sank deeper into the water.

"Hang on," a voice called. "I'll have you out of here in a jiffy."

With a sudden jerk Tigra was going up instead of down. Moment's later her feet touched the ground and the heavy wet sack opened on one end. Cold and soaked, she crawled out.

Standing in front of her was a strange creature like she'd never seen before. It had six legs, a hard reddish shell and huge claws that pinched at the air.

"That was a close one, kid," the voice said.

Tigra shook her fur, but it still clung to her body. "Thanks for saving me," she said. "Is there something I can do for you?"

"Nah," said the crab. "The sun will be up soon, and my mama is expecting me home for breakfast."

"Breakfast sounds good," Tigra said. "Can I join you?"

"Not unless you can breathe underwater."

Tigra shook her head. "No thank you. I've had enough water for a lifetime."

The crab pointed a claw up the beach. "There's Seagull. He sees many things flying high above in the sky. Maybe he'll know where to find food," he said, and then scurried sideways toward the water and disappeared into an oncoming wave.

Tigra shook her coat one more time trying to dry, and then scampered over to the seagull poking its beak in the wet sand.

"Hi," she said. "Crab told me you might know where I can find food."

The seagull glanced up. "Wha? ... Who are you?" he asked.

"I'm Tigra. A farmer tossed me into the water. If it hadn't been for crab, I'd still be in that sack floating out to sea."

The seagull strutted around the small kitten. "Hummm, I see, I see. You are a skinny little thing."

"Will you help me?" she asked.

The seagull raised a wing and pointed up the beach. "There's a rundown oyster shack not too far from here. Sometimes if you hang around the garbage cans, you get lucky."

Tigra thanked the seagull and headed up the beach.

In the distance, she saw a gray wooden hut with a straw rooftop and no windows.

She stopped and sighed. "Looks like nobody lives there," she said. "Maybe I should try another place." The words barely out of her mouth the scent of frying fish drifted her way. Wow, she thought. I've hit the jackpot. Her tummy rumbled, and she took off running toward the shack.

Tigra sniffed the sand by the garbage cans, but only discovered a few fish skeletons and a leaf or two of rotten lettuce. "Rabbit food," she grumbled. "There's got to be more. I smell food all around."

She leaped up the side of the garbage can, but slid down the slick metal sides onto her rump. Tigra tried again and again, but the result was always the same. Just as she was going to try one more time, a door slammed and a round-bellied man in a dirty white apron hobbled down a ramp carrying a large black bag. He lifted the garbage can top and dumped his package inside.

Tigra rubbed against his hairy leg.

"Hey, what's this?" the cook said, and then grabbed her by the neck. "Don't like critters hanging around," he grumbled. "If it can't go in my gumbo then I don't want it here." He held Tigra right up to his nose. "Wonder what cat tastes like in gumbo?" he laughed.

Tigra didn't know what gumbo was, but she was certain she didn't want to be in it. She squirmed and wiggled trying to break loose from his firm grip. But the cook held tight.

Seagull swooped down and pecked the cook on his head. Tigra tumbled to the ground, rolled head over heels. She found her feet and scurried away as fast as she could.

Fast wasn't good enough. Cook was right on her tail waving a meat cleaver over his head. His eyes burned with anger.

"You can't get away," he yelled. "I'm bigger and faster."

Tigra pumped her legs as hard as she could, but cook was right behind her. Out of nowhere Seagull swooped down, grabbed her by the neck with his feet, and flew high above the beach.

Cook hollered, jumped up and down shaking his fist. Tigra laughed and stuck out her tongue.

The higher they flew, the smaller everything became – the houses, cars, people and even the roads. Why, she was no longer a kitten, but a bird soaring in the sky. She liked being a bird.

Soon Seagull circled a thick grove of pine trees and oaks. He slowly descended toward the ground, and then set Tigra gently on a bed of pine needles. "No cooks here to put you in gumbo," Seagull said.

She shook her fur and licked her paw. "Thanks, that's a relief."

"No place is ever completely safe," Seagull said. "So be alert for danger, little buddy." He winked, then flapped his wings and took off.

Tigra waved and watched him disappear into the cloudy sky.

Now what, she thought scanning her strange new surroundings. Not knowing which way to go, she flopped down on the soft bed of pine needles and curled up in a furry ball. "So tired," she whispered. "I'll rest first, and then find food."

Thunder clapped, lightning streaked across the darkening sky. Large raindrops pelted the sleeping kitten's head. Tigra scampered to a hollow log a few feet away.

"Hey, who invited you?" a squeaky voice said.

Startled, Tigra humped her back, extended her claws. "Who's there?" She squinted her eyes trying to see in the darkness. As her eyes focused, red beady eyes glowed a few inches away, a long skinny gray tail swished across the log floor.

"You've invaded my home. I don't like uninvited guests," the voice snarled. "Get out."

"My name is Tigra. I've come a long way, and I'm looking for a home. Please let me stay until the storm is over," she asked.

"I don't like company ... particularly cats. Now git," the voice squealed, and then the creature nipped Tigra's tail sending her into the drenching rain.

"Better get out of the storm or you'll catch your death," a voice called from above in the tree.

Tigra shivered from head to toe. "I'd love to get out of the rain, but the only place I found was that log and the rat wouldn't let me stay."

"Just like a rat, always looking out for itself and no one else."

"Is it dry up there? Tigra asked.

"More than where you are," the voice said. "Come on up. Two warm bodies are better than one."

Tigra scrambled up the tree and climbed into a deep nest made of dried leaves, pine needles and twigs. She curled next to the gray bushy-tailed squirrel. "Hi, my name's Tigra," she said. "What a nice place you have."

"I'm Greta," the squirrel said sizing up the new occupant in her nest. "You a raccoon?" she asked.

"Why would you ask that?"

The squirrel studied her from every angle. "Well, you don't look like one of my cousins and you have black rings around your tail."

Tigra laughed. "No, no, I'm a cat."

"A cat? What in the world are you doing in the forest? You belong in a house curled up in someone's warm lap."

"Sounds great," Tigra said. "But there's no place like that for me. I'll just have to learn to be a squirrel or a raccoon."

Thunder rumbled and a stiff breeze whipped through the nest. Tigra shivered. Greta wrapped her bushy tail tighter around the drenched kitten, and then pulled more leaves on top of them. "Better?" she asked.
Tigra nodded. "Much better, thanks."

"Listen, sweetie," Greta said. "My friend Bandy *is* a raccoon. She has some human friends. Maybe she can find you a proper home."

"Do you think?"

"Yeah, I do. She and her four new kits visit the nearby farms most every night scavenging for food." The squirrel sat up and clapped her hands. "I bet she knows a good place you can live."

Tigra pulled Greta back into the nest and covered them with loose leaves. "Tell me later after the rain stops."

"No, no," the squirrel said. "This can't wait. I've got to find Bandy. You stay here and keep dry." With that, Greta crawled out of the nest and scampered down the tree.

Tigra snuggled deeper beneath the warm leaves and listened to the musical drops tapping gently close to her head. I'm so lucky, she thought. Not because I've lost my family, but because I've made new friends and have seen the world from high in the sky. I also learned that you've got to be able to tell who's your friend and who's your foe.

Her heart brimmed with happiness. Yes, she was one lucky cat. Moments later she slipped into a dream filled sleep of ruthless owls that helped heartless farmers steal families away. There were hungry, but helpful crabs who could only walk sideways, scary cooks with knives and boiling pots of gumbo. She dreamed of soaring high above the ground with Seagull by her side, and – –

"Hey, Tigra, wake up. I'm back," Greta yelled from the ground. "Come down and meet Bandy and her family."

She blinked her eyes several times, yawned and stretched. "That you, Greta?"

"Yes. Hurry, Bandy wants to take you to her favorite house. We think it might be just the place for you."

Tigra skipped her usual after-nap bath and scurried down the tree. Waiting for her were Bandy and four identical kits each sporting a black mask across their eyes and black rings encircling their tails.

"Hey, everyone," Greta said. "Meet Tigra."

Two of the kits romped over and examined her from head to toe. The others peeked curiously from behind their mother.

"Now, leave Tigra alone," Bandy said. "There's plenty of time to get to know her. But right now, she's hungry like the rest of us, and we have a long way to go."

She gathered her kits close by. "Now remember, always be alert for coyote. He's dangerous and means you harm."

"Coyote?" Tigra asked. "What's a coyote?"

"Coyote is devious, cruel and stalks small animals for prey. Sometimes he kills for fun ... sometimes he's just hungry ... but mainly, he's just plain mean." Bandy hung her head as tears trickled from her eyes. "Last year ... my family ... he ...." She dabbed her black eyes with her bushy ringed tail.

The words barely out of Bandy's mouth, an eerie howl swept through the forest. She turned to her kits and narrowed her eyes. "Heed my warnings and do exactly what I say." She glanced at Tigra. "That goes for you, too," she said.

"No problem," Tigra said. "I've been in enough danger for one day."

Everyone said farewell to Greta, and then she scampered quickly to the safety of her nest high in the tree.

As the five raccoons and Tigra trekked through the forest, the howls drew closer. Bandy rose onto her hind legs and sniffed the air. "He's getting close," she warned. "Tigra, you and the kits keep going straight ahead. Don't stop for anything until you reach the edge of the woods. Once you're there, the kits know where to take you."

"Aren't you coming with us?" she asked.

"I'll meet you later," Bandy said. "I'm going to double back and make a false trail for coyote to follow."

"But – –"

"I'll be fine. You just take care of my babies, and they'll take care of you.

Now, hurry so he'll lose your scent."

Before anyone else could object, Bandy headed back the way they'd come.

Tigra and the kits hurried along the trail until the trees thinned out and the forest gave way to a freshly plowed field. Staying as close to one another as they could, the five small animals struggled up and over the deep mounds of dirt. They moved closer to a light shining bright in the distance.

Soon Tigra and the four kits stood on the edge of a garden full of pumpkins, tomatoes and string beans. Bandy peeked around an oversized pumpkin and smiled. "What took you so long?" she asked.

The kits and Tigra piled on top of Bandy, screaming with joy.

"Enough, enough," Bandy said. "There's something I want Tigra to see."

She took the kitten into another garden, but this one had pink, red, yellow and brown flowers. Tiny purple pansies danced around her feet. In the corner, three candles rested on top of a large rock and flickered in the darkness. An old woman dressed in black knelt beside three graves.

"What's she doing?" Tigra whispered.

"That's Annie Eldridge, and she's saying goodnight to her loved ones. This is all she has left of them," Bandy said. "First her son was killed in Viet Nam, and then last year she lost her husband."

"Who's the third grave?" Tigra asked.

"Her faithful old cat, Shadow. He died of old age last month."

Tigra moved closer, but remained hidden in the shadows. "Does she do this every night?"

"Yes," Bandy said. "And when she's finished, she scatters puppy chow and marshmallows all over the deck, and then looks out toward the darkness and says, "Are you visiting me tonight, my little raccoon friends? You're all I have left.'"

A lump caught in Tigra's throat as she watched the woman perform her nightly task. I wish there was something I could do to make her feel better, she thought.

Bandy and her kits moved closer to Tigra and waited until Annie Eldridge was finished. As soon as she went inside the house, they raced onto the deck, and gobbled up the marshmallows first.

Tigra hurried after them, but left the marshmallows for the raccoons. She slowly ate her way around the piles of puppy chow scattered about the deck.

Bandy looked up from her dinner. "I bet if you went to her door she'd let you in."

"Have you ever been inside?" Tigra asked.

"Oh no," Bandy says. "We don't belong inside. We're forest creatures. But I have a feeling you're just what she needs right now."

"No thanks," she said. "I prefer being with you."

Bandy shrugged and continued eating.

The back door opened. The raccoons scrambled into the bushes. When Tigra looked to see what frightened her friends, she discovered the woman staring down at her.

"Well, well, well," Annie Eldridge said. "You're a strange looking raccoon." She reached down, picked up the kitten and gently stroked her fur.

Without realizing it, Tigra switched on her purring motor and nuzzled close to the old woman's neck.

"Would you like to come in?" Annie asked. "I bet I can find a nice warm bowl of milk, and I still have some of Shadow's tuna flavored cat food. That was his favorite."

Inside the cozy kitchen, Tigra licked the bowl clean. With a full tummy, she snooped around and discovered a warm fire crackling in a fireplace. Next to the stone hearth, there was a rocking chair and a basket of yarn and knitting needles. On the other side of the room there was a tree with twinkling lights and colorful shiny balls dangling from its' branches.

Tigra trotted to the tree, squatted on her haunches, and inspected the curious shiny balls. Her face reflected back at her. She laughed and batted the ornament with her paw. Mama, I bet you and my brothers *did* find a nice place to live too, she thought. The world is full of kindness if you just know where to look. Comforted by this thought, Tigra curled beneath the tree and began her after dinner bath. No mean old farmer was going to disturb her tonight.

Moments later, Annie Eldridge knelt beside the tree and gently scratched Tigra behind the ears. She folded her hands beneath her chin and looked upward. "Thank you, Lord," she said. "This precious little kitty is the greatest gift of all." Annie Eldridge stroked Tigra's fur one last time, and then picked up her knitting and sat in the rocking chair.

As soon as the woman was settled, Tigra jumped up and curled in her warm lap. From where she was laying, she watched Bandy and her family head into the darkness. "Thanks, Bandy … thanks, Greta," she whispered. "Because of you, I've found a safe place to live and a real person to love."

REG ALTAZAN

Last Thread

Third Place Short-Short Fiction

In a small diner in Manchac, Louisiana, Hal Kemp stood in a narrow hallway. It was paneled with creamy wood the color of caramels. There were coat racks on the wall made of polished cypress knees. The walls were hung with framed black and white photos of the diner, on the edge of Lake Maurepas. In one photo, he saw the front of the diner when it was new. There was the lake ringed with cypress trees, and the drawbridge a quarter mile away. Others were shots of fishing camps strewn along the bayous and marshes, stretching out from the lake toward New Orleans 40 miles away. The photos were from the 1920s. He noticed there were more cypress then. Other shots showed high water levels of one hurricane or another in the Fifties, Sixties and Seventies. Hal shifted his feet, lifting one then the other, and felt his weight on the concrete floor. He studied the floor, covered in beige speckled tiles laid out in the Fifties from the looks of it. There was a path where he stood, worn to gray from years of traffic.

He waited for the restroom which could accommodate one person at a time. He had heard the latch snap behind the man who got there before him. The door was old and even though he had not been inside, he could picture the old toilet, tile, and the funny sink with the plumbing exposed underneath. They all looked like that, these old places. He knew the glass light fixture was long gone and there would be a naked bulb in the ceiling.

These were the places his dad had favored long ago, when Highway 55 was the main road. That was more than thirty years ago, long before the interstate rose up over the swamp, dropping the fishing camps and diner into its shadow. He rode with his dad then, in the summer when his mother was too sad or confused to watch him. They'd drive the back roads, past tin roof shacks with scorched dusty yards, littered with appliances or cars, tired little towns with a clutter of buildings crowding a single main street or two, where his father would park his black paneled truck in front of the hardware store or local mercantile. It was in the front windows of such places that he would set up his display of sewing machines. There were Singer, Brother and cheaper no name brands.

The local women would stop to watch him zigzag or monogram. "You can't find stitching like this in store-bought clothes," he'd tell them. "Have a seat, give it a try." He would open up a little compartment on the top of the most expensive model and snap in a cam. The machine would stitch out perfect roses or stars, one after the other. "Look at that," the women would exclaim, gathered around the new sewing marvel, and all of them would want it. "Register for the free sewing machine. We'll be giving it away at five o'clock today," my daddy would say. The crowd of ladies would move toward the counter and fill out the drawing slips. They needed other things much more than that fancy sewing machine, but they wanted to win.

Hal thought of those little towns now, whose names he could not remember. He pictured the plain, small-town women, their hands red from canning or housework, knotted in excitement at the prospect of their name being called out to claim such a prize. He was hoping to stumble upon one of those places today when the rusting old drawbridge and diner called out to him from the interstate. This will do, he thought. He didn't want to kill himself in the city.

He heard the click of the latch on the restroom door. It ticked inward on its hinges. He stepped against the wall, avoiding the gaze of the old man who came out. As he entered the restroom, he turned to shut the door. He caught sight of the old man's dark blue shirt, swirling with some vague white pattern. He wore khaki shorts which swayed above small withered knees and leather deck shoes with blue socks sagging at the tops, around his thin shins, like the mouths of fish. He closed the door and leaned against it with his eyes closed and felt better as he slid the lock into the jam behind his back.

When he opened his eyes, he saw himself in the old mirror mounted between the toilet and sink. He watched himself as he pulled the bottle of pills from his pocket, poured them into his hand and then tossed them into his mouth. They were bitter and he had to cup his hands to drink from the faucet to wash them down. For a moment he thought he'd be sick and mess the whole thing up. He closed his eyes, leaned against the door, and took a deep breath.

When he opened his eyes again, he felt calmer and noticed the small jalousie window at the end of the room. It was cranked open slightly. Small streaks of light appeared between the narrow translucent rectangles of glass.

REG ALTAZAN

He was drawn to it and cranked the handle until all of the panes were horizontal. He could see dumpsters and a small outbuilding. Beyond that he saw marshes and the rusted hump of the old draw bridge. The marsh grass swayed as a warm breeze dragged over the tops of bushy patches. The mud was drying between clumps of grass and cracked, thick as fudge. He felt the heat rising from the metal dumpsters but could not smell them. He could taste the pills, or maybe it was the fine white dust, as it rose from the oyster shells in the parking lot. The air seemed wavy from the heat and smelled like a warm body.

He could feel the beads of sweat collecting on his forehead and felt another wave of nausea. He leaned against the wall, then slid with his back against it, until he was sitting on the floor. Its coolness surprised him. He closed his eyes and remembered the thin, hollow-eyed woman, who won the sewing machine. She had reminded him of his mother, the way she seemed smaller, when the weight of the unexpected event settled upon her. He had not known then, as they drove the woman and the sewing machine down the street to her house, that his mother would smoke a last cigarette, turn on the radio, and lie down across the bed. They would find her there the following night. He remembered how his daddy had screamed out her name, cried as if she had died that moment, and then cursed her.

Someone rattled the restroom door but Hal ignored it. He pictured the table where he had left his car keys. He imagined the waitress wondering where he was. He knew the ice in his glass had melted, and a ring had spread around the bottom of it onto the table. A man and woman near the windows ate crabs, cracking and sucking them noisily. The thin waitress backed into the kitchen, bent toward the weight of the tray of dirty dishes.

She had decided to buy a lottery ticket on the way home, and she had told him. And wasn't he just like her own son, slow to make up his mind, reading the menu twice. Hal had left a dollar on the table for her ticket. Maybe she was lucky.

November 22, 1963

Second Place Poetry

After school I walk home
Through the leaves piled for burning.
The schoolyard flag has dropped half way
Like a mailbox flag after the postman
Has left a brown letter.

My neighborhood is the empty
Street in a western
An hour before high noon.
I draw my six-shooter.
Leaves die in the wind.

I run through the house shedding my books.
My father is home this time;
His eyes are rifle shots.
Mother wrings her string mop hair.

I watch the news on TV.
I ask if Texas is a southern state.
No one answers.
I go outside and cover myself with leaves.

RONALD FRAZER

Kareem's Roti

Third Place Short Fiction

Marcus ate a dinner of saltfish, bread and cocoa tea with Agnita's four children, sitting on the rocks behind her shack looking west down the hill into the village of Victoria. Beyond the pastels of the village and the glare of the beach, the Caribbean was changing from mid-day turquoise to deep blues and oranges. Sylvia, his mother, left early that morning, telling the little boy to mind Agnita, a skeletal Indian woman who lived two doors away, and that she'd be home right after dinner.

Marcus enjoyed the street party that was customary every night after the dinner dishes were washed. The young men brought out boomboxes; one or two women made homemade ice-cream; and everyone gossiped, or walked up and down the road in the cool breeze calling out to the old folks sitting on their front steps. Marcus joined the other five and six year olds, chasing the goats, chickens and each other until sundown when the mothers began pulling them away one by one to scrub off the dust and sweat. When the last child was called, Marcus went back to his shack, took a bar of coconut soap from the table, and removed his tattered T-shirt and dirty peach-colored shorts. Wearing only his briefs, he went to the standpipe near Agnita's house to wash. There was a wait while two laughing women in frayed housedresses finished washing their naked toddlers. Marcus knew better than to jump in ahead of a mother at a standpipe.

After the women moved off with their children on their hips, he crouched down under the faucet using it like a tiny shower. The cool water and soap felt good as he rinsed off his day. Walking back up the hill to his shack, the trade winds blew from the jungle to the east chilling and drying his skin.

Back at his two-room wooden shack, he put on his other pair of white briefs and hung the wet pair on the string that his mother had nailed along the western side of the shack, facing the sea. He sat on the stone step on the east side of the shack, facing the jungle and the mountain, to wait for her. The party continued around the rum shop higher up the hill. The tsk-tsk beat of the Reggae was all that reached him; the rest of the music scattered by the trees and the wind. After an hour the eastern sky had become quite dark; he knew there'd be no more buses, so he went inside.

He wanted to leave a light on for his mother, just in case she was able to find a ride home, but he was too short to reach the matches where she kept them on the ledge at the top of the wall. Leaving the kerosene lamp unlit, he climbed into the creaking steel bed. He put his hand in the depression that her body left in the old mattress, and fell asleep remembering the feel of his hand on the great wall of her back and the smell of coconut soap on her skin.

He awoke disoriented in the morning. Sitting on the edge of the bed, he was about to call out when he remembered that she hadn't come home. He'd always awakened to the sounds of her moving around the house or clanging aluminum pots on the charcoal stove behind the house. He put on his T-shirt and shorts that had a little worn patch on the bottom where his briefs showed through, took a pink dollar bill from a tin on the table, and walked to the little shop at the top of the hill for some bread and cheese.

The lady at the shop ignored him while she served all the others — men who had come in to buy a single cigarette and girls who needed an egg or a pat of margarine for the family breakfast. When the shop was empty, Marcus stretched up to rest his forearms on the counter that ran completely across the shop dividing the customer waiting area from the stock. He held the dollar up and said, "Bread and cheese, please."

The shopkeeper, an elderly, rounded woman in a floral print headrag, took a loaf that was slightly larger than a hotdog bun, sliced it lengthwise and made a cheese sandwich from a few slices of oily cheddar. Marcus gave her the bill and wandered back home, nibbling as he went.

Arriving back at the shack, he sat on a rock across the road to eat the last bites of his breakfast. An ancient man passed on his donkey, his gardening tools clanking in a burlap sack tied to the saddle, with the air of a tiny general leading troops into battle, his back straight and his frayed felt hat cocked to one side.

The hours inched by with that imperceptible speed reserved for small children forced to wait. Marcus walked up and down the road playing with children from time to time but keeping the house in sight in case his mother returned.

About 4 o'clock in the afternoon, Marcus was sitting on a rock by the rum shop listening to the music and watching the bend in the road where his mother would appear. Two men were talking loud in the shop.

"Yeh man! De government truck hit dat woman, boy. De woman live in dat house dere."

"What house dat?"

The two men came out of the rum shop and one pointed at Marcus' house. "Dat house. You know de woman, man! She fat-fat, boy. She on de bridge in Grand Bras yesterday. De truck take de whole bridge. De woman broke up. She dead-dead."

Marcus looked from the pointing finger to his house and back to the man's watery red eyes. He decided the man was drunk. His mother had missed her bus, or the bus was broken down and they were fixing it today.

At dinnertime Marcus went to Agnita's house. He could see that she was staggering drunk. Snarling and grumbling about the extra mouth to feed, she gave him a piece of chicken and some breadfruit. Marcus ate, thanked her and went back to the rock across from his shack.

He didn't feel like playing tonight. He made marks in the dust with a stick and worried about his mother. The street party started up; the other children played around him, moving up and down the street in waves of bodies, chatter and laughter. Two young women stood in front of him for a while admiring a new baby. The crowd in the rum shop would explode with laughter from time to time. The reggae continued from several machines scattered along the road, each playing different songs. He decided to wash up and go to bed.

This time he was determined to light the kerosene lamp. He put the machete on the table, slid a rickety chair close to the table so he could climb up, then standing on the table he flicked the matches onto the floor with the tip of the machete. He sat on the chair, removed the glass chimney and struck the match. Smoke billowed from the wick as it came alight. Marcus turned the brass knob right and left until the smoking stopped, then replaced the globe.

For a few seconds as he watched the steady flame, he replayed, then rejected, the words of the man about his mother's death. Marcus turned and looked at the wall beside the front door. A rusted saw, spanner, and pliers that once belonged to his father were hanging from nails driven into the bare boards. He remembered his father's death two years earlier – the waiting for his father to return from the fishing areas that were so far out in the sea that the boats couldn't be seen even from the hill.

A round, tray-like gardening basket was in the corner of the front room. Marcus put the machete back in the basket where his mother kept it. An image of her slipped through his mind; she was carrying the basket on her head as she walked to her garden, holding the blade of the machete lightly in her fingers.

She would be home soon.

He went to bed leaving the lamp burning on the window sill so his mother could see when she came home. He told himself that she must be walking home. Her pillow still smelled of the earth, but the sheet no longer smelled of her body and coconut soap. He fell asleep.

A blast of heat and light woke Marcus. The entire front room was burning and flames blocked the only door to the bedroom. He stood on the bed and crawled out through the open window. Dropping onto the uneven ground, he lost his footing and rolled a few feet down the hill, ending up face down in the dirt.

People were already gathered on the road to watch the shack burn by the time Marcus walked past his burning bedroom and climbed up on the concrete retaining wall that kept the single-lane road from sliding down the hill. He sat there for a second or two but the heat was burning him. He walked across the street and stood with the crowd.

The neighbors on either side went to the standpipe to fill plastic buckets with water. As the flames grew, they sprinkled water on their own shacks to keep them from catching, but no one tried to save Marcus' home. Even had someone cared, it was beyond saving before the first voyeur arrived.

After an hour, the mumbling neighbors returned to their houses. No one spoke to Marcus. In his white briefs, with brown blotches of dust on the deep black of his skin, he sat on a rock across the street and watched the fire die. A few hours before dawn, he moved to the retaining wall and continued to stare at the glow of the coals and the little sparks that crackled and spattered. His mind was numb. He was too tired to think. Images of his mother and the inside of the house would wander into his mind for a moment or two, then disappear like a wisp of smoke leaving him staring again at the blackened wood.

As the sky lightened in the east over Mt. Standhope, the house was gone. A few charred boards that had once been the floor joists still smoked.

Marcus was hungry.

He went to Agnita's house when he saw her children come out to sit on the rocks for breakfast in the morning. Agnita was unconscious, but Helena, her ten year old daughter, built a fire in the little lean-to shelter behind the house and gave Marcus an egg and some bread for breakfast. Then he went back to the rock across from the burnt shack to wait for his mother. The Immortal trees on that side spread over half the road making a shady spot with a nice breeze.

Midmorning, the man who had rented the shack to Sylvia walked up the road. He beat Marcus with a switch pulled from a tree. Holding the small boy's wrist, he slashed at the exposed skin, leaving welts and cuts on Marcus' face, arms, back and legs. All through the beating, he grumbled quietly to himself about the stupid boy and the damned lamp. When he couldn't hold the boy off the ground any longer, he dropped the wrist and walked away leaving Marcus shaking, sobbing and bleeding in the dust of the broken road.

Marcus watched the man disappear down the road into the village. Just as the man passed out of sight around the curve, a whining, ancient Land Rover crawled into sight, zigzagging up the road as the driver carefully avoided the potholes. Marcus pulled himself to the side of the road and slumped onto his rock.

As his crying faded away, Marcus looked at the damage to the visible parts of himself. His sweat stung the scratches and cuts. It hurt to move but he knew he should clean up.

He saw Helena sweeping the dirt yard around her house. Marcus went to her because he'd seen her caring for her brothers after Agnita's beatings. Helena took him to the standpipe and used a bar of Detol soap to wash the dust, blood and soot from his bruised skin. She gently dabbed the trickles of sweat and blood with a cloth until the bleeding stopped.

Marcus stayed close to Helena for the rest of the day. Because it hurt to move, he mostly sat and watched her do her chores and care for her brothers who were both younger than Marcus. She fed them all and at sundown the four children slept in the ragpile on the bedroom floor.

Helena held him tenderly. Except for the slenderness of the girl's arms, it felt like his mother was holding him. Helena's little brothers were restless and talkative. Gradually they ran out of things to say and fell sleep. When Agnita came home from the rum shop, she stumbled into her bed still dressed.

The next morning an angry Agnita ran him off, "You tink I keep you, eh? You tink I got money? Got nothing for you, boy! Go, find you someplace! Go!"

Marcus hesitated. He had nowhere to go.

"Now!" Agnita snapped, taking a step toward him with her slapping hand raised.

Marcus backed away to get beyond striking distance. He looked at Helena's sad, sunken eyes. She looked back and shrugged her shoulders.

He walked down the hill into Victoria. All day he shuffled along in his little white briefs with the soot-stained bottom. He wandered around the places where his mother had taken him, standing for a few minutes at the door of the drygoods shop where she bought cloth, and lingering outside the grocery where she occasionally bought canned food. Mostly he watched the women getting off the buses from St. Georges. Several of them looked like his mother at first as he stood on the sidewalk looking up into the afternoon sun squinting to see their faces in the glare.

As the village quieted down for the night, he found a long-empty house with a wide set of steps in the rear. A dry mop lay on the top step where he lay down using the mop for a pillow. His skin was itching and sore. It was hard to find a position where a cut wasn't pushed against the rough concrete. He eventually slept for a few hours until the mosquitoes started biting him. It was hard to sleep after that. He'd doze off but the buzzing and the bites would wake him again. Around dawn he fell fast asleep.

He awoke midmorning, hot and hungry, having not found anything to eat the previous day. The sun was now shining directly on him. Marcus decided that there should be food near the main road. He went first to the women who sat near the Nutmeg Pool building where his mother sold her vegetables. He half-expected to see her sitting there with her lettuce stacked in front of her. A toothless old woman, sitting cross-legged on the sidewalk with her bananas and plantains, watched him for some time. He wasn't begging; he didn't know how. He just stood quietly looking at the food. She took a banana from a hand of ripe fruit that she was selling.

"Here boy. Take and go." She held out the banana.

Marcus took the banana and ran behind the building. It was a good size and filled the small boy. After a long drink at a standpipe, he wandered over to the beach, a busy and noisy place.

Some teenage boys were playing soccer on the sand; fishermen were dragging their skiffs up on the beach with the first catch of the day; and some young men were playing reggae on a boombox so loud that the buzz in the tattered speakers was louder than the actual music. It was a good place to watch the buses arriving from the capital.

Whenever a bus came into the village, Marcus would run over and stand by the conductor, looking at each face until everyone was off. Then he'd walk slowly back to the beach and sit on a crate in the shade of a shop.

By lunch time, Marcus' hunger was back. He returned to the market area where he noticed a Rasta with a roti stand made from bamboo and rough boards. He walked over and stood downwind of the stand so he could smell the curry. The Rasta was busy getting ready for his lunchtime customers so he didn't notice Marcus at first. Eventually he finished his preparations and slumped over the counter to wait, propped up by his forearms. It was then that he saw the little black boy standing at a respectful distance.

"Come boy. Talk to me, man."

The Rasta had made three tall stools for the front of his stand, one red, one yellow and one green. Marcus crawled onto the red one and gripped the edge of the counter with both hands.

"I hungry."

The Rasta looked at Marcus' bruised face and scratches. "You come to de right place, man! I make best roti in Victoria. Dey good-good, man! Everybody say so."

The Rasta put some potatoes and a little chicken in a roti and handed it to Marcus. "Easy man, it hot-hot."

Marcus nibbled slowly at the edge of the steaming pastry as the Rasta rambled, "Yeh man, Jah does provide all for we. Jah good-good to we. Jah make everyting you see, man. E-vry-ting! I-man give you roti, but it really Jah does give. Ras Tafari!"

Marcus had no idea what the words meant, but he liked the Rasta's wide, white smile and he liked that the Rasta was very dark like himself. Marcus smiled. He ate the steaming roti slowly, carefully testing each piece of chicken or potato to see how hot it was.

As Marcus finished the roti, the Rasta said, "Now, man. Is time to clean you mouth. You know dis bush?"

The Rasta laid a small stick on the counter, thinner than a pencil.

"Naa, man. I never see dat," said Marcus.

The Rasta brought out his cutlass and cut two pieces about three inches long. He handed one to Marcus. He pealed off the thin bark while Marcus imitated him. Then he chewed one end between his molars to fray the ends.

"Dere man. You chew and make brush to clean you mouth."

Marcus smiled and got off the stool with his new toothbrush in hand.

"You come back any time, man. Any time you hungry, Jah does give you more roti."

"Thank you."

The Rasta leaned over the counter and held out his hand, "No problem, man. I Kareem."

Marcus shook his hand, "I Marcus."

Marcus walked off toward the beach — down to the water this time to wash his skin. He took off his briefs and waded in until the water was across his chest. The water stung a few of the scratches so he washed quickly. He rubbed the briefs between his hands as he'd seen his mother wash them in the river so many times. He put them back on and climbed up on the keel of an overturned skiff to dry off in the sun, clean his teeth, and watch the boys playing soccer.

About two o'clock the government bus came up from St. Georges and stopped on the main road. Marcus ran over and stood by the door and looked at each woman as she got off. As the bus pulled away, Marcus stood on the emptying street, facing the sea while the passengers walked off in all directions.

He went back to the beach, climbed on the skiff and sat watching the soccer with his back to the sea and his chin in his hands. About 4 o'clock, another bus pulled up on the main road.

Marcus got off the skiff and took two hesitant steps toward the bus, then climbed back up on the skiff and faced the sea.

✭ ✭ ✭

Drowning by Proxy

Honorable Mention Short Fiction
(Chapter 1 from a Novel)

I was jogging up the dirt path to my house when beams of light burst through the pines, gilding the oyster shells underfoot and splashing colors on the bay. That moment always stopped me, the incredible surprise of the change from half-light to this brilliant display. I stopped, taking in the view, breathing in the fresh air. The resident ducks waddled into the Choctawhatchee Bay, upended themselves to fish, their occasional quacks harmonizing with mourning doves' calls; I winced when the morning paper slapped my front steps and a car pulled away. With a sigh, I tore myself away from the moment and stared at the newspaper, *The Florida Panhandle News*, lying on my steps unfurled like a telegram message I didn't want to see.

I picked up the paper and saw I had a reason to feel uneasy. The front page prominently displayed my ex-husband's file photo from five or six years earlier: high forehead, Slavic cheeks, deeply set eyes, small, tight mouth. Above it was the headline: "Navarre Developer, Cyril Smolensky, Disappears, Foul Play Suspected."

"What the . . . " I plopped down on the top step, my hands shaking. But why was I so surprised? After all, Cyril had "disappeared" in the past, mostly to mystify his family. Except that his maneuvers had never made the news.

I tried to find comfort in sunrays streaming through pine trees and dappling shadows under my feet. Ducks still quacked and boats chugged behind the house. Except that nothing was the same. Still shaky, I got up and let myself in, sat heavily on the couch in the living room and folded the paper so I could see the article better. I should probably get reading glasses,

MELITA GARDNER

but I could easily make out the picture of Cyril's beautiful sailboat, the Sea Sybil. It had been found stranded, its side badly damaged. I put the paper down, closed my eyes and vividly recalled the sky blue boat with a burned orange mast, lightly skimming the Gulf's emerald waters, Cyril balancing on the side tilted out of the water. To ride in that boat was the closest to flying I had ever experienced. Cyril knew how to handle a boat better than anybody else. He had loved it more than people, so if.... The picture in the paper was grainy, colorless, but I could feel the boat's violation as if it were my own.

I gulped audibly and opened the paper to find the rest of the story. The rustling of the paper brought in Trudi, my dachshund, who threw herself at me in ecstasy of greeting. I had no choice but to put the paper down to pet her, her rough tongue soothing my burning cheek. She tried to jump on the couch, something she wasn't supposed to do because of her back, so I picked her up. I didn't really want to find out any more of the sorry story, but when I glanced at the paper that flew open on page three, I think I let out a scream.

Inside, next to another picture of the wounded boat was a picture of my son Leo, stooped and disheveled. "Leo Smolensky," read the caption, "the eldest son of Cyril Smolensky and Marianne Lancaster, former Mrs. Smolensky, found the damaged boat. The local police are investigating his connection with the incident."

I crumpled the paper into a ball and flung it at the wall. My gentle son has never hurt anyone! "Anyone!" I shouted at the blank wall. Trudi yelped, but I just glared at her.

Anger pumped enough energy that I finally got up, retrieved the balled up paper and read the list of evidence against Leo. On Thursday, Leo had found the abandoned sailboat; witnesses reported Leo had struck Cyril six weeks earlier in a fight. Leo's clothes had been found on the boat. So what? I thought. Leo had gone sailing with his father.

My hands shook as I carefully folded the paper and put it on the coffee table, smoothing it. I walked to the picture window to calm myself with the familiar view of my back yard, ducks, seagulls and the shimmering water of the bay. When the view didn't help, I walked to the kitchen and fed Trudi.

I stretched. Nothing helped, so I started pacing. I knew how much Leo had to control himself not to fight his father, not to strike back. So if he had actually hit him ... Anything was possible. No, it wasn't, Leo wouldn't hurt anybody. He had had plenty of opportunities to lash out when he was teased in school—and he was, often. Even though he had been taller than his classmates, he had never attacked. "Gentle Giant," kids called him. Cyril's disappearance was probably a scheme Cyril had concocted to involve and maybe even frame various members of the family. He was capable of it, but I didn't know why. As usual, he was at least a step ahead of me. "Damn Cyril and his mind games," I muttered, then stopped. Just what I needed, a habit of talking to myself. Kids at the college already thought I was "kooky." Now I had to be more careful than ever. Since I didn't have tenure at Brandon College, the knowledge that my "ex" was the notorious Cyril Smolensky was bound to raise a few eyebrows in this Southern Baptist stronghold. My activities with the Citizens for Responsible Development were already suspicious.

I had come to the area with my second husband, Norman, when he was transferred to the Hurlburt Air Force Base in 1980, and most people around here knew me as his wife and then his widow, Mrs. Lancaster. Cyril had moved to Navarre a few years after me because the area was growing very fast and needed contractors. I could imagine Doreen, the English instructor at Brandon, my competitor at committee meetings and my frequent lunch companion; little Doreen with surprised big eyes would be the first to ask a lot of questions. The head of the English Department, tall, stiff precise and bespectacled Mr. Hollarn, was sure to lecture.

I suddenly realized Leo hadn't called for several days. In the past, I had been the first to know when Leo and Cyril quarreled. Leo knew he couldn't hide the story from me. He knew I read the newspapers. Did he understand he was a suspect? Was he even in town? For all I knew he had gone to Atlanta where his stepmother lived. Carla! Even though she hadn't lived with Cyril for three years, I could have laid a bet that she, her son Basil, or both were involved. Leo, of course, would be covering for them.

I spun around to grab the phone the instant it rang.

"Mom," came Leo's tentative voice. "You up?"

"Leo, are you okay? What happened?" I let out the breath I wasn't aware I was holding.

"It's a long story," said Leo. "Do you have time before class?"

"Of course. Come over. I'll make breakfast."

I sighed, wondering what to say to Leo. I had a talent for dealing with students, asking leading questions about their problems, but when it came to my son, I seemed to use a wrong approach most of the time. I should put on my everyday neutral face, I decided, and get ready for my nine o'clock class. I had to make sure I kept my job. And my sanity, I reminded myself.

Finally a hot shower thawed out my tight muscles, but my thoughts still raced. Cyril had taken Leo from me when I married Norman and insisted on accompanying him to the remote duty assignment in Korea. Cyril raised Leo. And Carla, I reminded myself. Actually, she had been more like a big sister, so he always took her side against Cyril and defended her children from their father. Leo refused to live with me even when the law would have allowed him to choose where to live because "the kids," Zoya and Basil, needed him. And every time Leo refused to live with me, my jealousy flared, the smoldering jealousy of a mother deprived of her son.

"I served a purpose too," I mumbled as I tamed my salt-and-pepper hair while still wet. How many times had Leo brought "the kids" over to protect them from Cyril's wrath? Scared kids, crying, Leo herding them like frightened animals. Leo's actions usually earned him the silent treatment from his father until I talked to Cyril because for some reason he listened to me. Cyril despised Carla, and her being high on some illegal drug most of the time didn't help. So I was caught in the slow family dance whether I liked it or not, all the while trying to keep my job and my sanity. Since I had survived Cyril up till now, I supposed there was hope. That was a bit like surviving fire and flood.

Bacon sizzled and I was cracking the last egg into the frying pan when Leo walked in. A firm believer in rituals, I knew a good breakfast would help us both collect our thoughts. Figure out what to do next. Leo leaned against the door jamb, his haggard face older than his twenty-five years, serious, looking so much like his father's I gasped: high forehead, unruly auburn hair, deeply set eyes and thin mouth. But that was where the resemblance ended. Cyril had steel-gray eyes, Leo my green ones; Cyril was barely five feet ten and Leo six-four. And Leo was messy, something Cyril abhorred. Leo's button-down shirt was rumpled as if he had slept in it, and I recoiled when I saw stains on his jeans. Probably refinishing my old chest, I reminded myself. Refinishing furniture and working with wood were his hobbies. His hair stood up in clumps. Like me, he raked his hair when under stress.

"Oh, Leo," I exclaimed. I walked over to him and put my arms around him, moved by his guileless appearance. He brushed his eyes with the back of his hand.

"Fresh coffee?" he asked in a grainy voice.

"I'll get you some," I offered, but the eggs demanded my attention, so Leo walked over to the coffee pot and poured himself some. Coffee in hand, he dropped into a chair at the kitchen table. When I put his breakfast in front of him, he smiled and gratefully inhaled the smell of fried bacon.

"This smell will always be you. Even when I swear off cholesterol," he said, patting his middle that bulged over the belt.

We ate in silence, I mostly to keep Leo company as bits of bacon stuck in my throat. Finally I pushed away my plate and said, "Okay, start at the beginning."

"I went to Dad's house six weeks ago last Sunday. He had called," Leo added quickly. "He wasn't home, so I went to the Fisherman's Dock on the Sound. Kinda mad he was giving me the runaround."

I nodded. How familiar, I thought, then asked, "Did you find him? What did he want?"

"Dad announced he had filed for bankruptcy. To hell with the business, to hell with the kids and to hell with Carla. He was moving. We had all conspired against him anyway."

"Moving? Where?"

"Oh, I don't know. He never got around to telling me. He ranted about children that turn into little con men as soon as his money is mentioned. About Carla's greed. Nobody can sue him if he's bankrupt, he says. He dropped the custody suit for Zoya, and he didn't care if he ever saw any of us. Then I slugged him. Right in his mug."

"You hit your father?" I asked slowly.

Leo nodded, sat up straight, and his eyes lit up.

"You should have seen his face. For the first time, ever, I saw him stunned, speechless. Can you imagine Cyril speechless? And with a paunch?"

"What, Cyril gaining weight?"

I couldn't imagine him either speechless or fat. I conjured somebody imperious, always in control, appearing taller than his five feet ten. The steel-grey eyes never flinched, always looked straight at the designated victim, mouth thin and tight. Only his birthmark in the shape of a claw would turn dark red. Had his eyes opened wide, unfocused, had his mouth dropped when Leo struck? All I could imagine was Cyril's flaring nostrils after the punch, that indignity which the man would not be quick to forget.

"It was worth it," Leo nodded.

"Leo," I tried to sound disapproving.

"Yeah, well, then he got really mad and pushed me into the Sound. By the time I got out, he was gone. I looked for him, but finally gave up and haven't heard from him since. At the time, I was glad I couldn't get my hands on him."

"I hope you didn't mention that to anybody. He probably went home and wrote you out of his will as he had done last time you took Carla's side."

Leo shrugged and said, "What difference does that make? All we'll get is debts."

He was right, of course. Leaning closer, I asked, "Any witnesses?"

"Seems like half the town was on the dock or in that little oyster bar. A few snickered. The cops, of course, know all about it."

I wanted to talk about the mess my son had gotten himself into; instead, I got up and put my coffee cup into the kitchen sink, then turned around and looked at Leo, scrunched up in the chair.

"Leo, why do you challenge him?" I asked for the umpteenth time.

"You've got your life. Just walk away."

"Some things you don't walk away from," Leo sat up, his hand in his hair. "His kids deserve more than just beatings. I don't give a damn about his sudden paranoia. Whatever we feel about him, he had it coming."

I turned away, knowing my son would never stop defending Carla's kids, no matter what it cost him. Or me. All I could do was help him figure out what Cyril had in mind this time. I sighed. For starters, several things in Leo's story sounded phony. Cyril had been suing Carla for custody of their twelve-year-old daughter for the last three years, so why would he suddenly give up?

"Leo, are you sure he dropped the custody suit for Zoya?" I asked. "You know he never gives up, just changes strategies."

"Oh, that was hopeless. Now that Carla is clean there's nothing he can pin on her to get the kid."

"Yeah, when your custody came up, I played into his hands."

I couldn't help my bitterness.

Leo walked up to me, put his hands on my shoulders and squeezed. I smiled. Never mind that old story. There were other parts of the new story that bothered me, like the bankruptcy. Cyril had put all his ambitions into the contracting business. The Florida Panhandle had been building up big time for a number of years, and Cyril had been born to build. I shook my head.

"Why would Cyril file for bankruptcy?" I asked.

Leo stepped away. He tried to explain how Cyril had overbuilt, took more credit than he could handle. Apparently he had mortgaged even Leo's property when Leo was still a minor and had not paid it off. Promised Leo he would sell the Sea Sybil. The rest of Cyril's properties, including his house in Navarre, were all mortgaged.

"So what was he going to do?"

"He wouldn't say. Called me square for worrying about money. And nobody else knows anything either. That creep Ernesto D. can't be found. I'll bet you anything his fingers are in the pie somewhere. He helped Cyril out during the hurricane four years ago."

"And he has been with Cyril since?"

"Yeah, one of his foremen until he disappeared. And Homer, the other foreman, doesn't know what to do. For some time now, Cyril shut himself off from everybody; he even gained weight. Homer tells me Cyril spent nights locked away. Brooding and eating."

"Cyril locked away? What's going on? He hates being alone."

"I know, and he loves to manipulate people," Leo looked at me. "My associate at the Infinity tells me Cyril bought one humongous life insurance policy with all the kids as beneficiaries. Just to create chaos when he dies. Mom, Mom, was he planning to die?"

His voice shook. I got up and took Leo's face in my hands. "Leo, he isn't dead. There's no body. Let's figure out what he's up to. As we've done before."

And suddenly those comforting words became a conviction I embraced, not just for his sake but for mine, too. But Leo didn't believe me. Hands in pockets, he pulled away and walked to the window. When he turned around, his face was composed.

"Leo, let's talk about the police. What do they have on you?" I asked.

"Yesterday I went to Santa Rosa Island to assess hurricane damages. It's already November, and Infinity Insurance has only begun. Can you imagine? Hurricane Ellen was two months ago. Anyway, I found the boat. Just lying there behind a wrecked house."

"How's that evidence against you?"

"Presumably I knew where it was," Leo leaned toward me, angry.

"What else?"

He straightened up but didn't look at me. "Mom, I swear I never took the hatchet to the boat," he said.

"What hatchet?" I was puzzled.

"The hatchet somebody hacked the boat with," explained Leo.

"How come the police divulged this information?"

Leo stopped his pacing and turned to me, his face even more haggard.

"To lean on me, Mom. You know the technique, I'm sure. Saying they know how deeply I'm involved so I'd better come clean."

I poured myself another cup of coffee and sat down. I was dizzy. "Have you talked to Carla? What does she say?" I asked.

Leo nodded, then shrugged and looked away.

"She thinks you got rid of him, doesn't she? For her, no doubt."

"Mom," Leo gave me an exasperated look, "she doesn't know me like you do."

"What do you mean? She raised you."

"Well, I'm . . . her champion."

"Great. And you don't have an alibi, do you?"

He shook his head. "The trouble is nobody knows when Cyril disappeared. He was last seen four nights ago when he sailed away."

"Who saw him?" I asked.

"A fisherman on the dock. It was like at eleven at night. On Sunday. Strange time for sailing even for Cyril."

"Do you have money for the lawyer?" I asked.

"My savings."

"So you'll need more. Are you staying here until I get back from classes? I've got to go."

His hand went to his hair. "Who wants to go home? Face the mess? Do cops always wreck a place when they search?"

"Probably."

"They brought along their dogs," Leo continued. "Sniffed out everything, the spare rooms, the garage, my car. Somebody let slip they were looking for dope."

"What dope? At your place?" I was really puzzled.

"I overheard a couple of them talking about something on the boat, crack, coke, I didn't hear right. So if they had found some at my house . . . Or even traces."

"Did they?"

"Of course not."

By now we were in the living room. Leo sank onto the couch while I proceeded up the stairs to my bedroom, but stopped on the second step.

"Drugs. If it's drugs maybe Carla's involved."

Leo shook his head.

"Or maybe Basil?"

Leo shot me a look and sighed, then shrugged.

I checked my watch. Half past eight already, so I told Leo, "Well, I'll be back by two. Call Carla and tell her she and the children are welcome to stay here. She and I have to talk."

He nodded.

Halfway up the stairs, I turned around and looked at Leo sitting on the couch hunched over. His hands dangled between his long legs. As if sensing my glance, he looked up and for a moment his bright smile and a shiny, soft look broke through the wall that was closing in on him. He waved.

Like Moses

First Place Short-Short Fiction

"I love your hair, Catherine," Cynthie says to me. Married to a Hollywood writer, she thinks nothing of flying cross-continent for lunch with her friends of almost forever. Inseparable from the third grade, all through college, we called ourselves, "The Four Cs": Cynthie, Chloe, Cheryl and me. I changed the spelling of my name from Katherine to Catherine to be part of the group.

The look on Cynthie's face, says someone, most likely Chloe, has kicked her under the table. For a long moment, no one says a word or risks looking at me, while I try to recall which wig I'm wearing today. I have five wigs, all different colors. It's my theory that the feature you take the most pride in will be the first to be taken away, but this doesn't necessarily hold true. I was always flat chested; losing a breast wasn't tragic. But my hair....

Cynthie often speaks before she thinks. We forgive her, she who values old friendships enough to get us together whenever she's in town. I sometimes wonder if she, like me, has so few friends that she must rely on the past for intimacy.

My real hair, black pepper with more than a sprinkling of salt, is nearly non-existent. What hasn't clogged my shower drain has likely washed out to sea. I visualize it tangled on coral, strangling small fishes, riding the waves all the way to Cape Horn. My counselor taught me to picture the chemo murdering bad cells, while the good are left to proliferate like rabbits. I also picture Green Peace tracing the hair back to me, the avid environmentalist, turning up at my door with stern warnings about my wanton pollution. I beg forgiveness and write them a check. I'm very good at visualization.

Cheryl has never been able to tolerate a lull in the conversation. "You look wonderful, Catherine. Much better than the last time we were together."

I try to recall how I looked last November. I nearly canceled out today, but when I awoke, today promised to be one of the rare good ones. If only it lasts through lunch.

"What does your doctor say?" Chloe asks.

My oncologist, bald as a melon, has no time to answer my questions as to why my hair has fallen out. He ignored me and frowned when he read my weight.

"He said I looked like a pre-pubescent boy and here I thought I looked like Twiggy." No need to explain who Twiggy is to this group.

I'm told Dr. Marcum is the best, but he lacks tact and humor, which would have been one of my pre-requisites had I a choice.

"I was set to tell him my wigs and bony body were all I had going for me, but I didn't. He wouldn't have understood."

What he would have done was suggest that I enroll in one of the clinic's support groups and I might have, if only they had one for smart-mouthed, bald, anorexics, suffering rampant malignancies!

It's too early to sass my doctor. I'll wait until he speaks the unspeakable, tells me I'm terminal. To appease him, I promised to eat.

"I guess Dr. Marcum's just waiting — like I am." It's an evasive answer but mostly true. Statistics say "one of four." I look around our table and wonder *Why me?* The answer is obvious: *Why not you? Your luck ran out. The other's didn't.*

The waiter has grown politely impatient. We order. Of course, I'm not drinking. I've nursed a tall glass of sweet tea for an hour. Cheryl pours the last of the wine in her glass.

Chloe mentions the obvious. More accusation than observation. "You're drinking."

Cheryl shrugs. No twelve-step slogans today, not until she decides to quit again. I see Cheryl's "on again, off again" bouts with sobriety as more addicting than booze. She craves the attention, the drama. It's what she has left.

Mercifully, Cynthie changes the subject, gives a glowing report of her recent retreat. The latest California "get-happily-ever-after" guru.

"Who's that?" Chloe asks.

Cheryl takes her chance to retaliate. "God, Chloe, do you live on another planet? He's on all the talk shows? You'd have to be brain dead not to have heard of him."

The word *dead* floats in the air along with Cheryl's cigarette smoke. I quit smoking years ago, but this moment I decide I may start again. What could it possibly matter?

I take a bite of shrimp and a fork full of lettuce that threaten to gag me. I swallow once, twice. Then again. My diet this past week has consisted mostly of crackers with a splash of Tobasco. I so crave anything with taste. Twice, I've thrown up—but then I've vomited dry toast.

I concentrate on the conversation: Snatches of political arguments, two are Republicans. I can't imagine that this has happened. Cynthie, coming from California, is a loud liberal. Me, I'm not sure I care anymore. Cheryl says there's a sale on silk pants suits at Bloomies' and we should go shopping after lunch. Then the talk is of the children, although most of the "children" are "going on" thirty.

I report my daughter, Audra, is amazing: Journalist. Wife. Mother. Next it's husbands. I can relax. I've been divorced for twenty-two years. Cheryl's Robert may, or may not, be having an affair. Cynthie's spends all his time working. "Might as well be having an affair with a woman," she says, "instead of his computer." Chloe's Tom is considering early retirement, an idea she plans to veto at the appropriate time.

"How's your mother, Chloe?"

"She's doing well."

We all know the woman could die any day. She's tended by Hospice, but Hospice is not to be mentioned in my presence. I arrange a pair of pink shrimp on my plate so they lie curled around each other, spoon-fashion. I remember it's how my lover and I used to sleep. I hope they can't read my mind. It's Tim for whom they reserve their ire. I've tried to explain that Tim is Tim, with limited patience for poor health or responsibility.

I wish he could have been more of what I needed and I curse him, too, but I curse jars I'm too weak to open, and that makeup can't conceal pain. Lots and lots of things. One especially bad night, out on my balcony, I cursed the moon.

Someone in a nearby apartment shouted, "Are you drunk?"

I, who had not had a drink in a year, screamed back, "Yes, Damn It! What are you going to do about it?"

I sip the last of my tea, push away my salad, and, at last, find something to say. "Can you believe? I saw on TV it's forty years since the Beatles were on the Ed Sullivan Show."

"Lord, I read that, too. My first thought was it can't be."

"We were all at Chloe's house, remember? Almost peeing our pants, waiting to see them."

"They were so beautiful in their little black suits and bad haircuts...so young, but God, so were we."

Cheryl sighs wistfully. "My Beatle was Ringo."

"Mine was Paul and he's still going strong." This from Chloe. It so like her to have chosen the most enduring one.

I won't mention that my Beatle was George. Too sad. Too ironic.

"Forty years? That's damn near Biblical. Like Moses wandering in the wilderness." Cynthie says "We can identify with that!"

Chloe frowns. "Speak for yourself, Cynthie. I've raised three good children, been married thirty years. I've hardly been wandering."

"The promised land," I say, "wasn't that what we were expecting? We thought life owed us that."

There's music inside my head. *I believe in yesterday.*

All eyes are on me, hoping I won't continue. This is lunch, after all, not a confessional.

I fall back on a comforting cliché. "But, isn't it the journey that counts?"

"Amen," Cynthie signs off. Cheryl lifts her empty glass. Chloe reaches for my hand and squeezes it.

Cynthie grabs the bill. For once, we don't argue. We each leave a tip — twice as much as required. Outside on the sidewalk, we hug extra tight. Four fairly attractive middle-aged ladies, each wondering if there will be a next time.

We walk away. Soon, I'll call a taxi when my strength gives out. I think about Moses and the promised land. The Sunday school stories. In spite of some heartbreak, because of the joy, I've loved my life. I hate to lose it.

But when the time comes — if it soon does. The music inside my head grows louder. John and George will be waiting. *They want to hold my hand.*

✳ ✳ ✳

The Lean Acres Chronicles

Third Place Non-Fiction

To describe my move to Lean Acres as unplanned, is more than an understatement! My wildest dreams had sometimes flirted with a place of my own in an idyllic country setting, but the move to Lean Acres was more like a forced exile to Ile du Diable! Six years of a martial situation had prepared me for a life alone, but somehow I had envisioned a more gradual transition to a place with at least a few creature comforts. I was not prepared for Lean Acres!

Lean Acres is the name of a small town near the border of Alabama and Florida. It's located about halfway between Crestview, Florida and Florala, a small town straddling the Alabama-Florida line. Lean Acres has a post office. In the last city council election, a total of 56 votes were cast, which immediately raised allegations that some folks voted more than once and some of the voters might have actually risen from the dead to vote. Lean Acres is surrounded by gentle rolling hills. The countryside is checkerboarded by alternating soybean and cotton fields and small tracts of pine trees. The primary industry of the area is poverty. With my decidedly hostile separation agreement, I fit in nicely.

Before I moved to Lean Acres, I lived in a tranquil neighborhood in Crestview. The comfortable houses were set on large, well-manicured lots, and the stately dogwoods and azaleas gave a country estate look to the surroundings. This was upper-middle class living at its best!

The day before the move was rather cold and bitter for an April day in northern Florida. The sun occasionally popped out for a few moments to try to chase the chill away, but it was soon stuffed back into a sack of clouds by the whistling remains of a March wind that didn't know when it had worn out its welcome.

RONALD H. ALLEN

My spouse, Elizabeth, and I had been embroiled in another war of wills that came about after her friend Buffy made a careless remark a few days before. Buffy, in one of her spates of mindless chatter, had dropped some information that might have been pertinent five years before, but was totally outdated and useless to anybody now, except possibly Elizabeth. It was, at once, the spark that ignited Elizabeth's fury and the straw that broke the proverbial camel's back. It tossed quite a load on my back, as well, but we'll get into that later. One thing led to several others, and I suddenly came to my senses while stuffing clothing and a few personal items into the back of my battered pickup. I promptly putted out of the driveway and turned north. Shortly, I found myself parked on a little parcel of land near Lean Acres trying to get all my worldly goods into a 25-year old travel trailer. We had parked the trailer there a year or so before, to get the eyesore out of our upper-middle class backyard and to show the neighbors that we eventually had plans for our property in Lean Acres. While I was moving in, it began to rain. This was a very appropriate portent of things to come.

The travel trailer was old, and in poor repair. I'd like to find something good to say about it, but nothing comes to mind. The floor was quite waterproof; unfortunately, the roof wasn't. That meant all of the water pouring in couldn't get out unless you opened a door or knocked a hole in the floor. Actually, I didn't choose either solution. I used buckets - and pans - and cups - and towels. It rained for days. At first I feared I might drown, which is usually hard to do when you're inside a structure. I learned a horizontal version of the Limbo, which enabled me to move from one end of the trailer to the other without getting a stream of cold water down my neck. Fortunately, the trailer was only 20 feet long, so I didn't have far to travel, and this minimized my risk. Fortunately, I was too busy finding and servicing new leaks to worry about claustrophobia. I spent most of my spare time trying to clean the mold off my mildew.

After the rain stopped, it got really cold. I mean – really cold! The travel trailer had electricity of sorts. There was a heavy-duty extension cord, running to the trailer, from a temporary utility pole 180 feet away. If you turned on a second light bulb, however, the first one would dim perceptively. This was not a problem at first because I had no appliances except a dilapidated old "apartment-sized" refrigerator. Unfortunately, it ran all the time, so I had to unplug it at night in order to use my table lamp. My regular routine became plug in the refrigerator, go to work, come home, unplug the fridge, turn on the lamp - well, you get the idea.

The first cold night I had to improvise. That meant using my only quilt and blanket as my primary bed covering and supplementing them with two sport coats: one over my torso and arms, one over my legs. I shivered through the night surrounded by dank walls and carpet still saturated from the rain. It was not one of my better nights, but it was memorable.

The next day I tied a white flag on a stick and ventured back to Crestview. After a short palaver, I returned to Lean Acres with a couple of quilts and a warm terry cloth bathrobe. The coming night would be different! It certainly was. With my bed loaded down with thick covers, I discovered how the bottom pancake must feel, but I was warm! Actually, I stayed warm until I tried to move anything. Then the exposed body part would immediately send out the alarm that it was being exposed to freezing temperatures, and I would awaken enough to drag it back into the warm cavity it had formerly made in the covers, or I'd shiver and shake until I warmed again. Another long night, but it was much better than the first one.

The next morning I faced a new challenge. It was Monday, and I had to get up to go to work. I couldn't lounge in the warm cocoon of my twisted pile of bed covers. I shrieked as my warm feet encountered the cold, wet carpet. I yelled as my body was assailed by the freezing temperature inside the trailer. I did a pretty fair version of an ancient Indian chant and dance as I hopped around trying to get both legs in my pants as fast as possible. I figured I'd had a pretty good aerobic workout by the time I was fully dressed.

This was the first of several times that I found myself shaving while wearing a ski jacket. If you've never shaved with cold water from a plastic jug (since the trailer had no running water) while standing in front of a mirror that is being fogged by your breath, you have something to look forward to. To make matters worse, my hand was shaking uncontrollably from the cold, and I risked serious injury as the razor made periodic contact with random parts of my face. It's at times like these, the intelligent person decides to cut his losses – literally. So I stopped cutting and losing at the same time. I didn't exactly have a close shave unless you consider my brush with death at the razor's edge, but it would have to do. I'm sure my colleagues at work were alarmed by my face, which was covered by small red nicks and wispy patches of a two-day's growth of whiskers. I looked a lot like Yasser Arafat with the mange.

Shaving was only one of the exciting new adventures that awaited me in a trailer with no running water and hence no hot water. To partially remedy this situation, and to solve another serious problem i.e., hunger, I decided to purchase a microwave oven. I shopped carefully because when I left Crestview I didn't leave with my pockets full of money. They were full of bills, but they didn't have "In God We Trust" on them.

I finally found a small, white, sterile-looking affair at the local Wal-Mart. For $85.00, I made the first major appliance purchase for my Lean Acres chalet. After placing it on top of the crippled refrigerator, I faced my next crisis. Would the extension cord be heavy enough to handle the microwave oven? I approached the problem in a true engineering fashion. I turned off all the lights. I made sure the refrigerator was off. I crossed my fingers and turned on the oven. It hummed and hissed and appeared to work properly. Hot dog! I was in business! I placed a small foam coffee cup full of bottled water in the oven and turned it on. In a couple of minutes, I was shaving with warm water, and I felt as pampered as an ancient Emperor of China! Later I placed one of my $1.25 TV dinners in the oven, set the timer, and pulled out a delicious evening repast. Now I was cooking – literally!

Cooking was a never-ending challenge. I could only store three TV dinners in the small refrigerator's freezer compartment. Since I had to leave the refrigerator unplugged most of the evening, the dinners would partially thaw and get mushy. Later at night they'd partially refreeze and stay mushy. After a day in the running refrigerator (it never turned off by itself), they were still a little mushy, and when I placed one of them in the microwave – you guessed it – it was mushy. But it sure beat pork'n beans or potted meat. I guess that is was fortunate that the freezer only held three dinners. That way, I had a much smaller chance of being poisoned by my much-anticipated evening meal.

As I've mentioned, the trailer had no running water, a rudimentary electrical system, and, of course, no indoor bathroom. This presented an interesting problem all its own. I solved it, temporarily, by digging out an old portable toilet I used for camping. The tiny little unit was light and handy for carrying, but presented a rather small target. It did not encourage long bathroom breaks, and carrying a magazine to the bathroom was wasted effort. In fact, the little unit fit snuggly in the tiny bathtub/shower combination in the trailer, and you actually ended up sitting on the toilet in the shower if you absolutely had to go. The whole setup encouraged one to "hold it" rather than go through the ordeal of climbing in and out of the shower and then trying to perch carefully on the postage stamp sized sitting surface, which, due to some unusual local phenomenon (El Nino, I think), stayed ice cold.

Due to budget constraints, I learned to think in terms of interim solutions. For instance, I needed a new roof, water, a sanitary system, and an adequate electrical system. I also began to dream of a room, which I planned to add to the south side of the trailer. Something big enough to stand up in without hitting your head on the light bulb, and big enough to turn around in without skinning your elbows. I needed all of these "improvements" to be comfortable, but I could afford none of them outright. None of these things could be obtained in one fell swoop. There were several steps involved in reaching each of these delightful goals.

For instance, the first desired improvement was a dry interior. That meant the roof became top priority. I worked up several designs, but they all failed the "dollar test." I couldn't afford them. I kept cutting corners, here and there, until I finally came up with a design I could eventually squeeze into my budget. It wasn't something that would excite Frank Lloyd Wright, but it got my juices flowing! The problem was that I would have to wait a couple of months before I could afford the materials, and in the meantime, it was raining about every other day. I elected to try the first short-term solution, which was to patch the holes and suspect seams in the roof with duct tape. This I did at the first dry moment.

The next day, when it rained, the leaks were diminished, but some were still there. The next step was to reseal the areas with more duct tape and then cover the spots with some cheap roofing sealant I'd eked out of my TV dinner funds. This worked so well in the light rain of the next day that I reinforced my repairs with another layer of tape and sealant. This was a much better (cheaper) answer to the leaking roof problem than spending big bucks on a more extensive repair. Eventually, I'd cover the roof, but what I needed now was a good two-to-three month fix.

The next couple of days it rained and rained. About fours hours after the heavy rains started, the leaks reappeared. I started setting buckets, cups, etc., again. This was getting discouraging. I'd spent more time on the roof lately than I'd spent inside the trailer, and it was leaking even worse than before. After the sun came out, I climbed up on the roof and found that the roof sealant was nice and rubbery in the areas where rain ran off quickly. But in small depressions where water tended to stand, the sealant eventually became water-soluble, which doesn't make for a good water repellant surface. My taping and sealing had actually made things worse because I'd torn the old tape and material from some of the seams and had replaced them with duct tape and my new handy-dandy sealant. In those areas, the soft sealant was allowing the water to pour into the interior of the roof in great torrents, and I'm lucky the entire trailer didn't just melt into the landscape.

Undeterred, more or less, I decided I'd have to cut more corners in my budget, and invest in the materials to cover the roof. That seemed to be the only remaining option. I needed the money now, so I had to take some drastic actions. After leaving the convenience store and ditching the rubber knife and stocking cap, I picked up the materials I needed to construct an entirely new roof over the trailer. The design no longer called for a lot of the framing I couldn't afford, especially the crossbracing, but I figured I'd put a good slope on it and the rain would drain well anyway. I spent a day, with Elizabeth's and my daughter Crystal's help, and put the shiny new roof on the trailer. It was beautiful! We all agreed that this was a roof to be proud of.

I could hardly wait for it to rain again. I anxiously leapt outside and considered the rain potential of each passing cloud. Finally (in a couple of days), the forecast called for rain. I lay on my bed and waited for the rain to start dropping onto the new metal roof. I remembered the sound of rain on the metal roof of my grandparents' house, and I warmly anticipated hearing that comforting sound on my own roof! It was a heady experience. It continued to be heady until the rain had fallen for about thirty minutes. Then I heard the ominous sound of water hitting carpet. I glanced back through the trailer, where days before I'd had to look through several small waterfalls, and noticed a couple of leaks. How could this be? We had just placed a completely new roof on the trailer! It was inconceivable that the roof could be leaking! But it was. My chin dropped to the floor and so did my spirits. I'd have given up but I didn't know where to go to surrender. I resignedly got out my pots and cups and started to finger my razor absently-mindedly.

When the infernal rain finally quit, I was on the roof in a flash. The problem was obvious. The unbraced design allowed the weight of the water to bend the metal panels downward. That left large puddles of water trapped near the edge of the roof, and at every point where the water level was higher than the joints between the roof panels, it leaked. I suddenly realized the trailer was predestined to leak. I could have welded stainless steel panels over the entire roof and the rain would probably blow in a window or somehow work its way up through the tires. I would never have a decent roof! I immediately went to the library and checked out the most useful book I could find, "Favorite Expressions of Inebriated Seamen," if I couldn't fix the roof, at least I'd learn to describe it!

After the initial shock of finding that a new roof doesn't guarantee a leak-free roof, I started trying to figure a way to fix my design flaw. I decided to slip a thin board under the roof from each end and raise the low areas from underneath. This would have worked fine, except one of my money-saving design changes had been to reduce the size of the framing members to the point I didn't have enough clearance to slip anything thicker than a fishing rod under the roof in the needed areas. I referred to my library book frequently during this repair effort.

Next, I decided on a fix related to the "mountain and Mohammed" solution. If I couldn't fix the roof from the bottom, maybe I could fix it from the top. I placed long boards on top of the panels and screwed wood screws through them from the top into the panels below. This pulled the panels upward and decreased the sag in the low areas considerably. This looked like it might work, so I gained new optimism. After I finished the job, I drew back and admired my handiwork. This was certainly thinking outside the box! I laid the book aside for the time being.

The next rain would be proof of the pudding. I waited apprehensively for the rain to return. I'd allowed my hopes to soar too many times in the past. Now I was skeptical of any fix until it proved itself. While waiting for the weather to cloud-up, I checked some of the trailer wiring that probably had gotten wet during the duct tape days. I turned on a small overhead light, which glowed dimly, but reassured me that the circuitry was still good. I did notice a small bead of sweat on the bottom of the light globe, however, so I decided to remove the globe and clean it. Maybe that would brighten the output as well. When I removed the last screw holding the globe, about two pints of water fell in my face and down the front of my shirt. The bulb had actually been under water when it was turned on earlier. No wonder the glow was feeble! After this startling discovery, I started backtracking the leak that caused the globe to fill. Apparently, water had been coming through the roof and flowing on the inside of the ceiling panels. This provided a nice path for the water to accumulate at the lowest available spot – the light fixture globe. Now, of course, that wouldn't happen again because I had fixed the roof, and the troublesome leak would not return.

During the next rain, much to my delight, the leaks had diminished considerably. There was only one small leak. This was major progress. I could now set a large cup under the leak, and would never have to empty it unless rain fell for several days. The only problem was that the leak was in the middle of the "living "room," and I couldn't stretch out my legs without intercepting the periodic drip. It was also hard to remember the cup and keep from knocking it over as I wandered about the spacious trailer, but this was much better than trying to run a gauntlet of several pots, pans, and cups that I'd used to catch the earlier drips. The final repair to the roof included sealing all joints with tough, fibered sealant. This discouraged leaks at the few remaining low points on the roof and sealed all the places where I'd punctured the roofing with wood screws to pull the panels up to the wooden boards on top.

Finally, I had a roof that I could trust to protect me during the heaviest downpours. I had persevered! Man had triumphed over Nature (and his own ignorance). I had met all challenges, made all possible mistakes, recovered from them, and finally had a dry abode. I'd also picked up several colorful phrases that quite adequately described the nature of roofs and roof repair.

DARLENE DEAN

HOMELESS

Honorable Mention Poetry

Brakes squeal. The world stops.
Bicycle wheels wobble in the air;
a wealth of cans strewn about.

A crumpled form,
motionless in the street.

Important someones exit
their steel sanctuaries.
They inspect but do not touch —
he's not one of them.

No time to think. Just act.
An inner force carries me there.

I sit at the edge of my world
drawn to the careworn stranger
whose face is like gnarled driftwood.

His craggy, weathered fingers
clutch my hand.
A toothless smile, his gift to me.

Life drains away on
my pale linen suit.
His eyes, seeing nothing,
stare back at me.

Tears streaming, blurred emotions.
I hold a lifeless form.
One small act of kindness,
too late to matter.

The Old Woman's Song

Second Place Children's Fiction

The old woman rocked slowly back and forth as she watched the moon rise over the sea from the window of her tiny cottage on the cliff.

Sea foam flowed onto the beach below. The tide was rising to greet the moon.

And as she sat there considering her life, which wasn't so bad, but was not always so good either, she began to notice a rhythm in the creaking of her rocker, and the gentle lapping of the waves on the shore. Her husband snored softly in his bed in the corner of the room, and the wind carried a simple melody as it whistled up the cliffside.

She began to hum while she composed a song in her mind, and when she had the words in the proper order and the rhymes in the right places, she began to sing.

Upon my toe
A bunion grows
It pains me morn to eve.
And if I had a wish tonight
I'd wish that it would leave.

But were it gone
'twouldn't be long
Afore I felt the pain
of my corns and warts and
my fallen arches
And so I'd still be lame.

The old woman chuckled to herself as she continued to rock, and the minor troubles of the day seemed to drift away in the wake of her silly song.

She must have fallen asleep, for she never noticed the tiny points of light that were carried into her cottage on the breeze. She didn't hear the tinkling speech that sounded like tiny chimes to human ears but was the musical language of the faerie. And she didn't know that her visitors had given her a gift in thanks for her song.

When she awoke in the morning and realized that she'd slept the whole night in her chair, she was angry at herself for doing such a foolish thing. Now she'd be so stiff she'd surely feel pain all the day long.

But she had to get up as her husband would be rising soon and would need something to eat before he went out to fish the sea.

Slowly and with care, she stretched first one leg and then the other. No pain. But surely she'd get a cramp when she tried to stand.

She tipped the rocker forward until the toes on both her feet touched the hard, cold floor. Then she pushed herself onto her feet, and winced her eyes against the pain she was sure she'd feel when her legs felt her weight.

Still no pain.

And as she took a step, something odd happened. Her shoe fell off. Her shoes that had always cramped her swollen feet before, were suddenly too big for her.

She bent and took a good look at her now bare foot, and couldn't believe her eyes. What she saw was a dainty foot, completely free of corns, calluses, warts, bunions, or any other such malady.

Her ankles were equally youthful, and upon further examination, she found that in only one night, her legs had lost years of age.

When she heard her husband begin to stir, she let her skirt drop back into place and quickly went on about her business. She prepared breakfast as she did every morning, but did it with a spring in her step this time, which was unusual for a woman as old as she.

After her husband had gone out to sea, she spent the day tending her garden without her shoes, so good did the warm earth feel beneath her bare feet.

It wasn't until the day was done and she'd settled once again in her rocker that she realized that though her legs felt fine, her back ached terribly from all the work of the day.

Once again she began to rock back and forth, picking up the rhythm and beginning another song.

I awoke this morn
with the pain all gone
from my legs and feet and toes.

*But my back still aches
and my hands still shake
and on and on it goes.*

*So if I had another wish
I'd wish and even beg
To have my spine,
which is old as time,
as strong as my new legs.*

And like the evening before, the old woman chuckled over her little song, and fell asleep in her rocker. And very shortly after that, the magical folk returned and left her with another gift in return for the night's song.

The next morning she awoke to find that she'd once again slept in her rocker. But this time she wasn't so angry with herself, for she noticed almost immediately that her back didn't ache as it usually did in the morning.

She sprang from her rocker and danced nimbly around the room, testing her legs to make certain they were still as youthful as they'd been yesterday. They were.

Then she bent all the way over, touching the floor with her lovely, slender fingers. She gasped in surprise. Her spotted and wrinkled hands with the gnarled fingers and swollen joints looked as young and pretty as her legs. And although she couldn't see her back, she knew it had changed as well. She hadn't felt so good in years.

Still she didn't tell her stoic husband what had happened during the past two nights, but fed him his breakfast and sent him out to sea. He was a solemn man in most respects, but he was also somewhat superstitious and leery of odd happenings, and she wasn't sure how he'd take such a change in her.

She finished her morning chores quickly, then fetched her basket and set off down the winding path to go to market. Any other day she would have dreaded such a trip, knowing that the trek back up the hill laden with a basket full of goods would have tired her out dreadfully. But today she fairly skipped all the way there.

Many of the townsfolk looked at her oddly when they noticed the way she danced from stall to stall, giggling like a lass of sixteen. Her youthful figure was covered by her long skirt and shawl, so they noticed nothing amiss there. It was generally thought that she was simply losing a bit of her mind with her advancing years for her face was as lined as ever.

She made all her purchases, and started her trip home, no more tired than she'd been in the morning. She even took the time to stop and pick flowers along the way.

That evening, like the others, she settled into her rocker after her chores were done and her husband had gone to bed. She thought about the people in the village, and how they'd stared and pointed at her antics, and whispered behind their hands. She rocked while her mind wandered, and soon she had the words for another song.

> *Would you look askance*
> *if I did a dance?*
> *Would you just see old and gray?*
>
> *Would you point and laugh*
> *and call me daft*
> *if I behaved that way?*
>
> *And if I were a beauty*
> *with pale skin and hair of gold,*
> *could I dance and sing,*
> *do anything?*
> *Would your gaze not be so cold?*

She sighed and closed her eyes, but sleep did not come so easily tonight, for her plaintive song had troubled her a bit, and she was restless from the day's activities. She was still awake when the faerie arrived, charmed by her latest song. She heard a sound like tiny bells jingling delicately in the breeze, and opened her eyes just a slit to see the twinkling lights floating in through her window. She thought she must be having a lovely dream, so she didn't make a move as the lights danced toward her face.

The little ones set to work quickly, weaving a spell around the old woman's head. Her skin began to feel warm as the magic touched her wizened old face, and her scalp tingled as the magic brushed through her hair. None of it brought pain, though, so she stayed still as stone, knowing that the faerie were shy creatures and would scatter in a blink if she disturbed them.

When the tiny people had gone, she jumped to her feet in search of the mirror she owned but seldom used anymore. She found it in the bottom of a basket filled with cloth scraps she'd been saving to make a quilt. She lifted it to her face with her hand trembling, and almost dropped it when she saw the beautiful girl staring back at her through the glass.

Even in her youth she hadn't been this lovely. The wee creatures had outdone themselves this night.

She was startled by a shout coming from her normally quiet husband. He'd awakened to find a strange girl going through his wife's things, and he was towering over her like a knight's angry steed.

"Thief!" he roared at her. "Leave those things be and tell me what you've done with my wife!"

"Husband, please! It's me. It's your good wife," she tried to explain through his rage. "I'm young... it was the faerie, they...."

He didn't give her a chance to finish as he advanced toward her. "Liar! Where's my wife? Have you harmed her?" She scrambled away from him, scurrying toward the door. Her terrified hands shakily fought with the bolt and threw it back, and she was out in the moonlit night and racing into the thicket before she had time to think what to do.

She ran for a very long time, deep into the forest, before she finally threw herself to the cold, damp ground of a small clearing and cried bitterly. What would she do? Where would she go? Her dear husband didn't recognize her, and even if he were to give her the chance to explain, he'd never believe that the lovely young girl standing before him was actually his wife. She filled the sleeping wildwood with the sound of her great, gulping sobs, begging for the faerie to come and help her, but none appeared.

After awhile, her tears began to slow and she took several deep, wavering breaths and somehow managed to quiet herself. She let her thoughts drift back over the past two days, at the wonder of waking that first morning with no pain in her legs, and then the magical healing of her back and arms and hands. She recalled the odd sensation of the tiny lights working their magic on her face and hair earlier that evening, just after her third song.

Her songs! She suddenly realized what it was that had called the little people to her before. They had loved her silly little songs. If only she could sing them to her side one last time.

She closed her eyes and opened her ears to the sounds of the forest. Crickets chirruped from every direction, while the leaves in the trees whispered quietly with each slight breeze that moved them. An owl hooted in the distance. She found the rhythm, and in a melodic voice that fit her pretty new face she began to sing.

Foolishly I sang a song
that wished for youth and beauty,
when all along
my needs and wants
were found in things around me.

Like my husband, long in years,
yet strong as the rushing tide.
I love the old dear
and I'm happy here
and I want to grow old at his side.

So Faerie if you hear my song,
Grant me one more wish.
Make me old
so I can go home
to my cottage upon the cliff.

 Faintly at first, but growing louder with each passing moment, the dancing lights returned on the breeze. They hovered close, but did not come all the way into the clearing. Realizing they would not approach while she watched in wide-eyed wonder, she closed her lids and breathed deeply and began to relax. She was exhausted from her flight into the woods, and before she realized it, she'd fallen asleep.
 She was awakened at dawn by the lovely sounds of birds beginning their day. She was sure the fairie had forsaken her when she realized she felt no pain from a cold, damp night spent in the forest. But as she reached out to push herself up from the dewy ground, her eyes adjusted to the bright morning and she spied in front of her the familiar sight of her gnarled old fingers and liver-spotted hand. Never had she seen such a beautiful sight!
 When she heard the welcome sound of her husband calling out to her from a distance, she leaped to her feet and ran to greet him, nimbly jumping fallen logs and dodging low-hung branches. And as she threw her bony arms around him, and pressed her wrinkled cheek against his, she didn't even spare a moment to notice that though the little people had given back her wizened old body, they'd not returned any of the pain.
 The faerie watched silently from a nearby hollowed-out stump covered with the ever-renewing growth of healthy green flora, and they were satisfied that they would have the old woman's lovely songs for many years to come.

✷ ✷ ✷

DELORES MERRILL

Sonya Renay Was in the Paper

Honorable Mention Poetry

It's true what we read
She had another kid her Mama said
This one dropped in the neighbor's yard.

Mama wrestled her five foot nine
Cut the cord with a fish skinnin knife
It's true what we read.

She screamed red spread
Soaked the ground cause
This one dropped in the neighbor's yard.

Mama yelled picked him up
Dirt crusted skin almost white
It's true what we read.

One breath a small sigh
No tears from tiny shuttered eyes
This one dropped in the neighbor's yard.

I need ya'll to come Mama said *I don't want to be alone
With fifteen candles and no cake.*
It's true what we read
This one dropped in the neighbor's yard.

A Cat's Tale

Honorable Mention Short-Short Fiction

Two months ago my girlfriend Amy left me to join the Air Force. Since the barracks didn't allow cats, she left Pouf with me. She said, "Oh, don't be so sad, Peter. You sit at your computer all day, so Pouf is all the company you need. I know you'll take good care of him."

So now I sit in front of the screen, while Pouf sits on top wrapped in his oversized blue-gray tail and stares at me cross-eyed. Suddenly he jumps off with a grumpy meow, threads himself around my chair and nudges me with his nose.

"Want out?" I ask and get up.

But no, he stands in front of the open door, hunched up and hissing. I can either choose to ignore him or try to figure him out. Sometimes he nibbles at my heels, leaps at the curtain, takes off and launches himself at an area rug, certainly not the model Persian The Cat Fanciers' Association describes.

Maybe he is just of superior intelligence and suffers from boredom, so I look online for a companion. I explore all possible combinations: pet mate, mate for pet, pal for pet, friend for pet, lonely cats, etc. Nothing. Exasperated I punch in "help a cat" and, zap, a listing appears. When I click on it, vivid blue color liquefies the screen and bright letters announce the site will list my pet and if a matching companion is found in my vicinity, it will let me know. I lean back and turn to Pouf, who, as if on cue, swivels his owl-like visage at me and stares.

Two days later, a note appears. A match has been found with a female Persian named Pompom who lives in my subdivision. Since the site supplies the phone number, I dial. After a bit of whirring on the other end, I hear a click.

"Hello?" I respond.

After some quiet breathing, a quivery "Hello " floats in.

I launch into the introduction. "Mrs. Purdy, I understand you have a Persian cat named Pompom. The Internet site 'help a cat' lists her."

"Y-y-yes," comes the reluctant answer.

"Have you just listed her?"

"Um-um," is followed by a chewing kind of noise.

"Mrs. Purdy?" I prod.

The woman is suddenly all business. "What's your name?"

"I'm Peter Capucci and have a male Persian I would like to mate."

"Oh, a boy for my Pompom," quavers Mrs. Purdy. "What kind is he?"

"A Himalayan, with a darker nose."

"I suppose we could arrange a meeting. I'll call you back tomorrow. What's your number?"

I give her my number, and we hang up.

The next day several notices appear on telephone poles and fences announcing the disappearance of pets. The security guard at the gate is alerted. In our community greyhounds and Shar-Peis, Chihuahuas and poodles run around at all tim,es of the day and night. Even purebred cats are allowed outside, and my Pouf often has the opportunity to look down his blunt nose at a neighbor he considers inferior. But now, pet owners give each other suspicious looks as they walk their pets, and only alley cats prowl the streets.

Since I won't let him outside, Pouf develops an attitude. He follows me around or crouches by the door. A couple of times I have had to chase him down the block. His purr has taken on a guttural quality and subsides into a strangulated gurgle.

I become really concerned when Pouf's behavior takes a nasty turn. I find yellow spray behind the study door and when I scold him and take him roughly to his litter box, he hisses at me. He sharpens his claws on furniture he has forgotten existed. One day, as I am designing a home page for the new veterinarian, I hear Pouf making all kinds of ungodly noises in the living room, so I sneak out to see what he's up to as he takes a leap at my curtain and claws. I haven't declawed him out of deference to his manhood, just as Amy refused to neuter him. When I finally manage to reach him, I grab him by the neck and pull. I finally have him by the neck as he opens and closes those formidable claws.

I return to my computer and force myself to concentrate on the page I'm designing. The cats I draw all come out as dragons, so I finally admit to myself I have a problem, which I need to address. I call Mrs. Purdy. A bit of companionship or mating might calm the beast. Mrs. Purdy hesitates, claims Pompom's indisposed, but after a minute concedes Pompom is just nervous.

"The situation, you know," she explains. "Persians are so intelligent and delicate."

"Yes, I know," I agree, and we are invited to visit.

A frail old lady opens the door, suspicion written all over her wrinkles. Beside Mrs. Purdy stands a small-boned cat with fur that is more silvery than gray.

"Pompom, I presume," I smile at the cat. I would like to say something about the exquisite beauty of the creature but don't want to make the woman suspicious. I do worry about Pouf's size in comparison. How could Pompom accommodate him?

Mrs. Purdy smiles at him, and he strains at his leash. "What a big boy. And how handsome."

She leans over to pet him. He suffers the touch and even purrs. So let her pet him all she wants. I'm offered tea in a porcelain cup while the two animals are served Fancy Feast in miniature goblets. Pouf cleans his dish right away and turns his attention to his new friend's portion. She ignores him and keeps eating in her dainty way until he tries to push her nose away. She doesn't even lift her head but utters a tiny hiss, at which Pouf backs away and sits down. I wonder. Mrs. Purdy immediately refills his goblet.

"This will give his coat a beautiful shine," she informs me and keeps admiring Pouf.

I feel like apologizing. "I didn't know..."

"How old is Pouf?" she asks.

I admit I don't know.

"You mean he is not registered?" the woman says raising her eyebrows.

"Well, I think Amy—my girlfriend—may have registered him, but I'm not sure."

"Amy who?" she asks.

I mention Amy's last name and tell Mrs. Purdy our story.

"Well, maybe he isn't even pure-bred," she concludes and her smile reveals a pair of sharp canines.

I shrug. The pedigree interests me not a bit, just the welfare of the beast. And my sanity. As if to reassure me, Pouf sits contentedly, licking himself, then flops over and meows in a most endearing way. Paws crossed, he rolls on the rug and squirms. The crone turns to me and tells me he is just having a good time. "He is starved for company."

Or maybe the Fancy Feast was laced with catnip. I decide it's time for us to go home.

Pouf disappears a few days later. I walk around with fish sticks in pockets until my coat smells. When the collars of the other lost pets turn up in an alligator's belly, Pouf's navy blue collar with a silver trim is not among them. Somebody has seen a coyote stalking the neighborhood, but my Pouf is too quick for him. Amy is very concerned, too, and joins me on my walks whenever she can. Pouf is still alive somewhere, we comfort ourselves, so we hang up notices, put a word out on the "help a cat" site, offer a reward in the newspaper. Nostalgia takes me to Mrs. Purdy's house, but the place is dark and blinds are drawn.

Weeks pass and I still wander around looking for my Pouf, alone. I wonder if Mrs. Purdy has moved for Pompom's sake. On my walks, I often stop to watch an alley cat wash herself, so when I see a small gray cat grooming her kitten in the window of a new brick house, I stop. The cat raises her head and looks up, then lifts her delicate paw to her tiny tongue. Pompom! Do I dare find out who the kitten's father is? When I ring the doorbell, Mrs. Purdy opens the door a crack and sticks out her head.

"Ye-e-es?" she looks at me and is about to shut the door, but it is too late. I notice a damp yellow spot on the wall by the door and behind her, on a little table, sits my Pouf licking his oversized blue-gray tail. He stops for a moment and stares at me, the old bored look replacing a brief spark of recognition. With a smug meow, he jumps off and disappears toward the window with Pompom and the kitten. I wave good-bye and walk away, my steps finally brisk as they used to be before Pouf came into my life.

✻ ✻ ✻

Too Old

Second Place Short-Short Fiction

"I am an old man bent with age," he says, "and still I dig."

I listen to only this part of their conversation and then I walk over to my workplace. What he says is not poetic simply because he wants it to be. Age is not poetic. It is not immediate or passionate or pitiable.

For me, it means that as I rake I do not sweat as much as I know I should. I sweat like a showerhead with intermittently plugged up holes and low water pressure. Age means that I rake with a back that grows stiff against the progressing sun. It means that I have learned to bend slowly even when I am not bending to pick up something heavy.

And it is late in the day now, so when I bend, I steady the rake beside me and sink down against it, priding myself on the fact that I can support my weight on my heels. But I know, too, that this makes me the old man, bent with age.

As I kneel, I sift, and I know that the newspaper reporter moves slowly toward me, his notebook still open. He walks the base of my trash mountain, carefully avoiding the perimeter. He reminds me of a young child walking along the beach, one eye on the moving tide running out of his way to avoid the inevitable encroachment on his path.

"Hello," he calls, this child on the edge of a sea of trash. He yells as though my gray hair is a sign of a defective hearing aid.

In fact, we have all learned to hear selectively, to ignore the drone of massive machinery and listen for the higher pitched, irregular tone of another human being's speech. We listen especially for the sound that is the highest pitch of the speaker's voice. That sound that indicates discovery, triumph. And we have heard it, and those near have followed the discoverer as he runs, suddenly energized, toward the detectives. But he has always been wrong and sometimes embarrassed. And after several of these mistakes, each of us has taken simply to walking to the detectives alone and silent.

But still we listen for the voice.

The reporter waits until the nearest bulldozer backs away and then he calls again, even louder. So I stand, kicking the darkened newspaper, frozen food cartons and diapers in front of me. I carry my rake, leaning on it a little as I walk. I reach the reporter, and he takes a step back to maintain between us a slightly greater distance than normal, even between strangers. I watch as he checks the impulse to wrinkle his nose, and I am surprised that he can distinguish my smell from the general stench of the dump. I try to hide my smile.

He is a short, balding white man in running shoes, jeans and a button-down shirt. His face holds the polite sweat of those who have never done manual labor. It is beaded slightly on his bare upper lip and his forehead, as if he wishes to communicate his understanding of our plight by sweating a little alongside us.

His glasses reflect me, and I see that I am a white biohazard suit and an air mask distinguished from the others who crawl over their own mountains only by my hair color, my stature. I lift off the air mask.

I am aware that the reporter has said something, but I am not aware what it was; and I know that if I am silent he will repeat it. And probably louder.

In high school Spanish that falters more than he realizes, he asks me why I am here. I know that this is the repeat and that before I took off the air mask he said it in English.

"My son told me about it. He is a police officer," I answer in English.

"So you have children yourself?"

"Yes."

There is a pause.

"Mr. Rivera, the police detective told me that you get up at 4:00 a.m., and you drive 70 miles one way to be here," the reporter says.

I watch as a line of sweat appears from underneath his sunglasses running down his face and in a huge drop off his chin. He wipes away the path with the thumb that holds his pencil, probably believing more from instinct than experience that his gesture will make it harder for more sweat to follow.

I smile as I am reminded, oddly, that with me bursts of emotion sometimes cause involuntary trickles of tears, among other things. But I am no longer surprised or disturbed by this.

The reporter continues to look at me.

"How hot is it today?" I ask him.

He waits several seconds and the pencil relaxes in his hand. "It's almost 100 degrees."

I look at the mountains of trash, vast and colorful beneath the monochromatic and brilliant sun.

The reporter follows my eyes. "The others say they hate to think of it," he says.

I know that this is his last attempt to get me to speak. I nod, but I do not look away. "We are looking for a boy in a pair of black jeans, size 29, a black button-down shirt, a white T-shirt, paisley boxers, black tennis shoes with red laces, an Armitron watch," I say. And then I lower my head before looking back at the reporter. I know his pencil is still because he already knows this information.

"I taught statistics at Arizona State," I continue. "I can tell you that all these things amount to the smallest fraction of a percentage of the trash in this dump. We work all day and we go through 400 tons of trash, but we search so little of what was dumped that day from Phoenix. Time and the heat work against us — the boy has been here for six months. That's why we have a forensic anthropologist, not a doctor or even a medical examiner."

"But if you don't think you'll find him, why do you do it?"

I open my mouth for a second, tempted by the reporter's invitation. "Hope. Because this is no way to be buried." Or, more academically, "Because we seek to reaffirm life by honoring the dead. The search is more important to the living than the discovery would be to the dead." But I shut my mouth before I give voice to the words. I am too old to be trite, unnecessarily verbose or vague. If I am still alive years from now I will know why I was here today looking for the body of a murdered boy I know only by his death. But that will be because I will forget the disappointment we feel when we bring the detectives a Mickey Mouse watch, not an Armitron, blue jeans instead of black. I will forget how forgetful we are in our eagerness. I will forget that I could not sleep the night after I brought the forensic anthropologist a bit of bone and she said it was a turkey.

The reporter waits awhile, staring in my face and then looking away. I know he wants me to move forward, or at least to pretend to for his sake if not for my own.

Instead I shrug and look toward my mountain and the place where I was standing before he came to talk to me.

"Do you know it was his friend who killed him?" I want to ask, because he didn't. But he does know.

I lower my air mask. And so it is two boys we look for.

✵✵✵

MAUREEN VREELAND

Something's Under the Bed

Honorable Mention Children's Fiction

What's under the bed? I know something's hiding there, no matter what anybody else says. My mother tells me it's just my imagination. What do mothers know? She looks under there and sees nothing but fluffy, gray dust kittens. My friend, Harold, told me the dust is really a person. He said he heard it in church. The minister told everyone, "Remember you are dust, and unto dust you shall return." Harold thinks he's so smart, but he can't even tell me if the dust under my bed is a person starting or ending.

Anyway, after my mother gets the vacuum and sucks up the dust kittens (the bodies) from under my bed, she smiles and says, "There. Now there's nothing under your bed."

Does she really think I think the thing under my bed hides in the dust? That's just baby stuff for little kids. When you're in second grade, like me, you know better. Grown-ups can be so dumb sometimes. I guess that's one of the, ah, occupational hazards of being adults. I'm not sure what that means, but I heard my older brother say it, so it must be true.

Maybe you're wondering how I know there's something hiding under my bed. Well, sometimes I hear strange sounds in the night. No, they're not creaky, old-house-at-night sounds. I told you, I'm in second grade now, and I know the difference between those noises and strange sounds. The things I hear come from right underneath me, like they're just under the floor but not downstairs in the dining room. I figured it out. There must be an invisible secret hiding place between my floor and the dining room ceiling. I'm not sure what kind of creature lives there, but I KNOW something does. Maybe there's even more than one of them, because some nights, like when the moon's full, it gets real noisy in there. That must be when there's a monster meeting or maybe a party. Those noises don't scare me like they used to. I mean, if a bunch of monsters are having a meeting or a party, they're gonna be too busy to worry about chasing kids, but....

If I tell you something really private, will you triple promise not to tell? Well, when that creature under my bed is all alone and he starts making those creepy monster sounds, SOMETIMES I get a little bit afraid. I mean, what if he gets hungry in the night and decides he wants a midnight snack, and there's nothing in his 'fridgerator? Even though I'm in second grade, I'm not quite big enough to fight off monsters yet, and my big brother can't help me, 'cause he doesn't even believe me about the monster under my bed. Sometimes big brothers are as much of a pain as grown-ups. But when I get a little bit bigger, like prob'ly when I'm in third grade, the very first time I hear those weird sounds at night, I'm gonna climb right out of bed and look under there with my magic flashlight, that's the only way you can see those monsters, and I'll laugh right in that guy's face. That will make him disappear, 'cause monsters hate people to be happy, and the only way they can really scare you is if you let them. That's what my grandpa told me, and he knows everything.

Shh. Do you hear that? Wow, that monster is really loud tonight...

Maybe I'll wait till I'm in fourth grade.

Good night.

✷ ✷ ✷

DELORES MERRILL

An Investigation of the Hermaphroditic Influence in *AS YOU LIKE IT* and *CYMBELINE* on the Seventeenth Century Idea Of Woman

Honorable Mention Non-Fiction

It is early 1600 in London, and for most men and women there is little hope of escape from a dreary life of lingering plague epidemics, various diseases and harsh living and working conditions. But on days when the flag flies above the Globe Theatre, Londoners flock across the Thames to Bankside in anticipation of having the gloom of reality lessened for a time. It seems that Shakespeare, major dramatist and part owner of the Globe, is the popular arbiter of what most audiences want to see on the stage. The Bard is certainly writing in his element when he constructs two plays that not only revolve around two women in similar circumstances but also seem to appeal to the senses in more ways than one.

Rosalind and Imogen in *As You Like It* and *Cymbeline* must be admired for all they undergo in their respective forests. But because of seventeenth century theatrical conventions, are we seeing the characteristics of bravery and endurance applied to the idea of real women? If a convention is a way of viewing human nature on the stage that becomes a bond between playwright and audience, then the idea of the seventeenth century woman as represented in the two plays could be disparaging, unattractive and discouraging, if the women in the audience accept the idea as reality.

Shakespeare borrows the character of Rosalind from Lodge's popular novel and thrusts her on the stage of the Globe in situations considered comedic and calls it *As You Like It*. Ten years later, in another of his theatres, Blackfrier's, Shakespeare produces one of his last plays, which is an arrangement of the legend of Cunobelin, a king of the Dark Ages, and his disobedient daughter, Imogen. He surrounds the daughter with melodramatic circumstances akin to those of the exuberant Rosalind and puts her in the romance play, *Cymbeline*.

In *Cymbeline*, Imogen escapes from imprisonment in Britain and has a temporary stay in Milford Haven in the forest of Wales. Her escapade begins with the advice-giving servant, Pisanio, who mistakenly poisons her and leaves her to the mercy of the dark Welch woods. Following Pisanio's urging, Imogen disguises herself as a boy, Fidele, so that she can move secretly about and observe her husband, Posthumus, who does not believe in her faithfulness. Pisanio, in Act III, scene iv, bids her wear the disguise and *tread a course pretty and full of view; yea, happily near the residence of Posthumus*. He warns her to *forget to be a woman* and instructs her to sound *quick-answered, saucy and as quarrelous as the weasel*.

In *As You Like It*, Rosalind also flees her surroundings with her supportive cousin, Celia, and a faithful court clown and also escapes to a forest setting. But instead of dark, mystical woods she ends up in the light pastoral Forest of Arden in France face to face with the love of her life, Orlando. Unlike Imogen, however, Rosalind makes her own decision to disguise herself as the boy, Ganymede, as she says in Act I, scene iii,

> *Were it not better because that I am more than common tall, that I did suit me all points like a man? A gallant curtle-axe upon my thigh...in my heart lie there what hidden woman's fear there will...and a swashing and a martial outside...*

Even though Rosalind seems more confident in her quest, while Imogen's confidence becomes undermined by the independence of her situation, it appears that both characters are self-assertive females as they take on disguises for self-preservation in the masculine-controlled world of the woods. This means that both roles must be characterized by strong-willed portrayals in order to determine the idea of what might be termed selfhood in the seventeenth century female with a reconciliation of her desires and circumstances. Could this idea of selfhood be Shakespeare's perception of the nature of woman? Could this mean that the audience perception of the seventeenth century woman is influenced by Shakespeare's fictional females?

If some magical device could realistically assemble theatrical conditions of the early 1600's and obviate the modern perspective of the stage of that era, perhaps it would be possible to extract a true nature of the idea of woman and her desires from the expectations of the Elizabethan/Jacobean audience and expand upon the response. Since no magic is available to reconstruct playwright, theatre and audience, it is necessary to try to understand, through investigation, theatrical conventions that influence Shakespeare as he creates roles to entertain and assimilate short-term expectations by his audience as they live in the moment of the play.

Certain theatrical conventions would affect audience response to the performances because on Shakespeare's stage representation of the fiction of the female gender and its accompanying sexuality was assigned to boys. With the addition of the male disguises of Ganymede and Fidele, the boy actors portraying Rosalind and Imogen take on the old favorite of the English theatre, a drag act which then becomes double drag. Even though this may be obvious to the English audience, historical investigation cannot recover the subtle effects cross-casting would have in connecting character and performer to audience expectations. It may be possible in the early 1600's for a typical audience to watch boys dressed as girls, dressed as boys and accept gender personation as a theatrical convention that helps exhibit the actor's art. On the other hand, the performance of the boy actor may become an eroticized experience for some spectators, while an aesthetically distanced illusion for others.

It is because the theatrical convention only repeats the cultural practices of a patriarchal society in which women share disfranchisement with their children that the female character seems ambiguous. The convention is foregrounded in the social attitudes toward gender which impose femininity on boys and at the same time trivialize women's social roles. It celebrates female heroism yet excludes women from the economic and artistic opportunities of theatre. The boy actor playing Rosalind comments indirectly on this situation when he remarks in Act III, scene iii, that *Boys and women are for the most part cattle of this color.* At this point it does seem that Shakespeare's texts construct gender from a relentlessly androcentric perspective.

Some critics assume the interpretations of the roles are set on a celibate stage with focus on the absence of physical representation of sexuality. If so, this would further assert that Shakespeare has discovered the truth of both tragedy and comedy which lies beyond sensual bounds. This interpretation gives legitimacy to the male cast as female and the homoeroticism of the transvestite boy by emphasizing the formality or stylization of acting demanded by the all-male cast. In other words, transvestism can intensify the artifice of the Shakespearean stage and maintain that the boy actor is somehow more aesthetic, more central to the practice of theatre than a female actor. Seventeenth century cross-casting certainly seems to imply that tragedy and comedy lie beyond the sensual bounds of the female actor, even though the female is deemed naturally sensual because of her gender. It is an ironic situation that allows the boy androgyny the freedom to play the puns and tropes of homoerotic flirtation.

Even though the boy in the breeches role is the acceptable convention of this era, the actor's submerging himself into the part to present an individual character, rather than a generalized style of acting, becomes a new and challenging technique of the art emerging in the late 1500's through the middle 1600's. A look at two different scenes for the characters of Rosalind and Imogen leads to the assumption that both boys in the roles will push acting effectiveness toward the homoerotic as entertainment as they become the alter egos of Ganymede and Fidele.

Rosalind, in Act III, scene ii, is in the Arden Forest disguised as Ganymede, and meets Orlando, with whom she fell in love back at court. Ganymede vows to cure Orlando of his love *madness* for Rosalind and says, *I would cure you, if you would but call me Rosalind and come every day to my cote and woo me.* Orlando answers, *Now, by the faith of my love, I will. Tell me where it is.* This dialogue exchange can be interpreted as an association of cross-gender casting and homoerotic flirtation. On one level, the flirtation is between the two male actors who are playing Rosalind and Orlando. On another level, a fictional woman, Rosalind, is flirting with Orlando while talking to him as if she were the boy, Ganymede. On a third level, the dialogue describes a courtship game played between a boy and a male lover who imagines that the boy is a woman, thus elevating the double drag situation to triple drag! The wit and stimulation of the passage seems to enhance the ability of the transvestite boy to successfully negotiate a sexual liaison with another male. Poor fictional woman, Rosalind. She appears now as a simple mediator who allows homoerotic flirtation between two males.

For Imogen, in Act III, scene vi, the flirtation comes from an unexpected character. In disguise as Fidele, Imogen is discovered in the Welch woods by Guiderius, who does not know the *fair youth* is his sister. Guiderious says, *Were you a woman, youth, I should woo hard but be your groom in honesty. I bid for you as I do buy.* In this scene, the homoerotic flirtation between the male actor, Guiderius, and the male actor, Imogen, dressed as the boy, Fidele probably titillates the imagination of Shakespearean audiences as they escalate the situation to include incest. However, Imogen, as the female refers to Guiderius as a *friend and brother* and wants nothing more than food and a place to rest as the boy Fidele.

These flirtation scenes do seem to eliminate female interference, and focus on transvestite boys in sexually arousing situations with other boys or men. If the celibacy of the stage is maintained by omitting the presence of the female body and represents physical sexuality in the language, then the boy-woman exchange produces the sexual celebration of the boy in drag, whose language eroticizes his appearance. Shakespeare extends this transvestite flirtation to the audience as the boy actor who plays Rosalind delivers the Epilogue. The actor reveals that he is a boy and speaks directly to the audience, first with the women then with the men as he says,

> *...I'll begin with the women, for the love you bear men, to like as much of this play as please you; and I charge you, O men for the love you bear to women (as I perceive by your simp'ring none of you hates them), that between you and the women the play may please. If I were a woman, I would kiss as many of you as had beards that pleased me, complexions that liked me, and breaths that I defied not; and I am sure, as many as have good beards, or good faces or sweet breaths, will for my kind offer, when I make curtsy, bid me farewell.*

Even though Shakespeare allows truth about the actor's gender in the speech, the boy refers to his fictional gender and suggests he would kiss the men. But note he does not make any kind of flirtatious remark to the women in the audience as they are used only to *foreground the men as the objects of desire*. After his coy list of *good beards, faces, and sweet breaths*, the actor performs a female gesture as he curtsies then exits. It appears, therefore, the Epilogue illustrates that whenever Shakespeare's female characters in the comedies call attention to their own androgyny, the resulting eroticism is to be associated with their maleness rather than their femaleness.

Furthermore, this may imply that woman is thought of as another object of trade between men just as signs, goods, and currency all pass from one man to another. Rosalind becomes an object of exchange within a homoerotic economy created to allow the boy actor playing her to play a boy in his flirtation scenes with Orlando. The fiction is necessary to negotiate the taboo against homosexuality, exchanging it for the aesthetic of the stage. This makes all fictional females upon the seventeenth century stage the merchandise necessary to facilitate erotic exchange, the sex objects which mediate trade between two sexual subjects.

Puritan reaction against what they perceive as decadence of the stage is often related directly to this practice of the transvestite theatre because Puritans concentrate on clear gender distinctions and their relation to heterosexuality. *In Histrio-Mastix: The Players Scourge or Actors Tragedie of 1632*, Puritans record their perceptions that boys in the female parts encourage homoerotic responses by members of the audience who *have been desperately enamored with Players Boys, thus clad in women's apparel, so far as to solicit them by words and by letters...*

Even though Puritan documents cannot be considered as unbiased accounts, they do provide information about both homoerotic and misogynistic anxieties of the period. Several extant sermons are built upon a Biblical quotation from the Old Testament specifically forbidding cross-dressing because it is an abomination to God. Deuteronomy 22:5 states, *A woman shall not wear man's clothing, nor shall a man put on a woman's clothing; for whoever does these things is an abomination to the Lord your God.*

In 1583, the Puritan writer, Philip Stubbes, suggests in *Anatomy of Abuses*, that the boy actors are Sodomites, citing their *lewd adulterous kisses and embracements upon the stage*. Though these reactions may misplace the *titillation from language to physical behavior, overlooking the function of artifice*, they do record a perception that the homoerotic effect is used for the entertainment of the audience.

Dress codes of the era that prohibit cross-dressing, not only for moral reasons but also political, probably provoke special enjoyment for the forbidden from the audience. Certainly women in the audience might relish the adventures of Ganymede because they symbolically represent the woman willfully leaving her usual subordinate position to the male household member. Fidele's wanderings without a companion certainly transgress the physical limitations and boundaries placed on the female by society.

Is it possible for the seventeenth century woman to better appreciate the artifice of theatre by seeing boys in female parts? If so, then there might be some concern with the method in which the age understands female beauty when the female is portrayed by a boy. Do the women perceive the stage in the same light as the Puritans, that is, as homoerotic games? Do they become voyeurs watching the flirtations of Shakespeare's boys? What sense do women have of their own sexuality? Are women only sexual as boys? The doubling of cross-gender dressing first in *As You like It* and later in *Cymbeline* may encourage them to think that women can only woo and take part in sexual games as boys. After all, the plays do not necessarily illustrate the way in which heterosexual marriage confirms the order of society. Rather the endings seem to state that within Shakespeare's stage world males marry each other to produce a sense of narrative and dramatic closure.

Ironically, it appears that most feminist studies of Shakespeare in the last several decades, for the greater part, ignore the fact that the majority of plays are read textually without considering the practice of excluding women actors in cross-gender casting. Most works, concentrating on independent women in the comedies and contrasting them with the negative images of women in the tragedies, characterize Shakespeare's portrayals of women as ahead of his time or the best of his time. Can it be that Shakespeare has the ability to see through the limitations of conventional gender expectations, and his only motive is to provide a maturing experience for the boy actor playing female characters? Is this possible without deconstructing the powerful misogyny found in the image of a man playing the woman's role?

In reality, it is common knowledge that Shakespeare knows his audience inside and out. Because of financial and political difficulties along with recurring plague threats, London theatres close for 18 months as he writes *Cymbeline*. This means he has plenty of time to work with characters, situations and passions already explored in *As You Like it* and try to sharpen the particular, minute-by-minute atmosphere and expectations of his audience. For a while, as theatres reopen, Shakespeare's stage offers a kind of haven of cultural construction as the central concerns of the period concerning sexuality and the female gender are acted out. These elements seem safe within the artifice as the boy actor portrays the sex object, powerful in cross-dress, but basically dependent. With the permanent close of theatres in 1642, however, the safety of artifice is removed. Boys no longer represent women. It is horrific irony that at this time the unrealities of the cultural fictions which suppress women explode into the realities of witch hunts as women are being accused, murdered and tortured for the supposed sins of their gender.

When theatres reopen in the late 1600's, women are allowed to play the female roles in bawdy comedies and narratives of lust that are popular on the stages. Now the fiction of the female gender is applied to real women. This age of the woman actor marks a transition from the virgin goddess Athena and virgin queen Elizabeth to the sex goddess that appears to be continuing into the twenty-first century, perhaps more so with the increase in popularity of pornographic theatre. Either way, it seems, whether it is a choice of the woman actor or not, most do not escape the role of merchandise in the world of male exchange.

It does seem, however, that the idea of woman is continually being revalued. Thanks to the redefining feminist movement of the twentieth century, the boundaries of the female nature have been opened and are being understood in terms of greater inclusiveness and fluidity. Women remain in lead roles as women. In the seventeenth century, however, this cannot happen, especially as a result of feminism.

The twenty-first century idea of how the seventeenth century stage convention affects the idea of woman is most likely influenced by the modern stage that admits liaisons between two male lovers as well as between women lovers. In Gay and Lesbian theatre, for instance, the characters tryst with characters of the same sex with or without the artifice of cross-dressing. Unlike what happens on the seventeenth century stage, this same sex liaison leaves no doubts in the minds of the audience as to the sexual orientation or intentions of the homosexual actors.

In speculating on reactions to a Shakespearean play by the average seventeenth-century female, it is perhaps safe to assume that reactions probably do not reach proportions of a highly philosophical nature. Men in the audience may guffaw and walk away from the performance thinking that most women are not as handsome as young boys just seen on the stage. While the average woman, not especially attractive because of being overpowered by the burdens of her gender and the realities of a short, painful life filled with hard work, probably saw herself, if she even considered a comparison, far removed from the fantasy world of the fictional females, Rosalind and Imogen. History tells us that the majority of women of this era live demeaning and undignified lives, dying in childbirth or of untreatable disease. They have no vote, few rights and choices, and most all are illiterate. They die without knowing that divine hermaphroditism is available to be believed in.

Because of their real, unfictional lives, therefore, it is probable that women in the seventeenth century see boys on the stage as nothing more than adolescents cavorting in female dress rather than a disturbing conflict to the idea of femininity or serious threat to views on sexuality. It seems safe to assume that Shakespeare's convention of cross-dressing is accepted as stage artifice by women, and they view the flirtation scenes as a desired fantasy which interrupts dreary routine and offers an entertaining respite to unromantic lives. They probably accept Rosalind/Ganymede, Imogen/Fidele as real women and do not question their sexual orientation, either because they do not think of it or because it would be pointless to do so.

A brief note from the Publisher

There are many elements to master in the craft of writing. Our skills are put to the test each time we consider plot, theme, characterization, scene and structure, dialogue, conflict, and action. The list goes on and on.

Like any professional, we must hone our skills; and so we study - a lot. We learn from the master teachers such as Dwight Swain, Orson Scott Card and William Noble. We also study the works of popular writers to gain a better understanding of techniques and of the markets. But the bottom line is this: we simply must write. And it is often times such a lonely business.

Another way to grow is by entering contests such as was held for this volume of *SandScript*. The contest was open to members and non-members; finalists were chosen through a blind-judging process by a qualified panel of professionals (no contestant information was available to the judges). It is a great demonstration of the caliber of the ECW organization to see so many of our members as finalists in *SandScript Volume II*.

One of the endearing traits of the "writers' cult" is a willingness to share knowledge, techniques and advice with fellow writers. The following two contributions were generously provided by the authors at our request to further round out *SandScript Volume II*.

The first special feature, "Habits," was provided by Jeremiah Healy, a long-time writer with many published credits. He gives generously of his time as a frequent workshop presenter and volunteer for numerous board positions in a variety of writing organizations. You can learn more about this prolific writer by visiting his website: www.jeremiahhealy.com.

Vision, up-beat attitude and tenacity are the underlying traits of any good writer. Our Founder and outgoing President, Julia Schuster, used those same driving forces to take the seed of an idea in 2000 to form Emerald Coast Writers, Inc. Without her undying commitment and support, this group would have never come to be.

As she steps down to again concentrate on her writing, she will be greatly missed. Words cannot convey the numerous ways in which she has touched so many lives. And so it is with great pride and pleasure, that we have chosen her as our second featured writer with her non-fiction piece, "Fruitcake Cookies and Bringing Mother Back to Life." Learn more about our founder at: http://juliaschuster.tripod.com and on our website: www.emeraldcoastwriters.org.

Let us hope that the rest of us can continue the dream and follow honorably in her footsteps.

Keep writing!

"To read without reflecting is like eating without digesting."
– Edmund Burke

Habits

*Special Feature
Short Story*

"As my brother Earl would put it," said Joe Bob Brewster from the rocker on his porch, "you're having a day of bad bio-rhythms."

Chief Lon Pray looked up from the window of the town police cruiser at Joe Bob, a paperback book open in his lap and a sleepy hound dog named "Old Feller" twitching his tail under the chair in time to the rocking of his master. Pray couldn't recall ever meeting Joe Bob's brother, who'd moved away before Christmas a year before, but he had been introduced to a couple of the Brewster sisters, and they varied from Joe Bob's carroty hair and stocky frame about as much as one pumpkin from another. Unfortunately, though, issues of family-tree—or Yule Tree—weren't what brought Pray back to Joe Bob's dusty front yard for the second time that December morning.

The Chief said, "You still haven't seen anything, then?"

"Uh-unh," from the man in the rocker.

"You ain't turned up nothing from all those roadblocks?"

"Nothing like the three that hit the bank, anyway."

"Well," said Joe Bob, "I sure didn't hear them running down behind the house here," flicking his head to the rear.

Three men, in masks, had hit the bank just as it opened that morning. Pray had seen his share of armed robberies while working as a detective on Boston's force up north. But instead of a getaway car with a wheelman out front, these guys had run across the street and down a path through the wooded hillside half a mile above Brewster's ramshackle home. They'd apparently stashed a pick-up truck on a fire road about midway down the slope, because the one witness who'd had the courage to run after them saw it pulling away in the distance when he reached the fire road himself.

Only thing was, Pray had contacted his patrol units within two minutes after the bank manager had called it in, and the county sheriff within two after that. This part of the state—which Pray had found himself just by driving south from Massachusetts one brutal February until he started feeling warm—had paved routes laid out like a grid pattern at intervals of roughly three miles, so setting up roadblocks had been both practiced in the past and easy in the present.

Except that while quite a few pick-up trucks had been stopped, none had contained three men, their handguns, or thirty-six thousand in cash.

"Besides," said Joe Bob, "Old Feller would of tore them to pieces."

Pray tried to refocus. "What?"

Joe Bob seemed hurt, leaning down to scratch his dog between the ears.

"Old Feller got wind of three strangers barreling in here, Chief, he would of tore them to pieces."

"Right." Pray tried to keep the sarcasm out of his voice, especially given that he hadn't seen the hound burn twelve calories total in the five months he'd been driving past the Brewster house to the restaurant where he took most of his meals.

"Well, if you do see or hear anything, call the office."

"You gonna go around to everybody else you already talked to once?"

"Can't think of anything else to do," replied Chief Lon Pray, putting the cruiser in gear and pulling away.

* * * * *

"Like I told you before, Chief," said Mary Boles from behind the bank desk, a nice holly wreath centered on its front. "It had to be somebody who knew we had extra cash on hand to cover the mill's Christmas bonuses."

Watching Boles—a plump black woman in her forties—Pray fidgeted in the "customer" chair, finding it uncomfortably like the "client" chair in his divorce lawyer's office back in Boston. "Isn't that pretty widely known, though?"

"In town, yes. Even in the county. But robbers from any distance away? I don't see how they could know that today was one of maybe three times a year there'd be enough cash in the vault to be worth stealing."

From Pray's experience, armed bank robbers were the most dangerous felons around exactly because they didn't know very much, or plan very well. But, he had to admit, so far these had planned well enough to fool him.

"Mary, can we go over what happened in here this morning?"

"Again?"

"Please?"

"Okay." The manager seemed to compose herself for reciting a particularly distasteful poem. "I'd just opened the front door from the inside, and Eugene was just unlocking his drawer at the teller's cage, when the three men burst in."

"And Josh?"

Boles blushed at the bank guard's name. "In the bathroom, like I told you before."

"Then what?"

"These three men came busting through, like they knew the precise moment I'd be opening up."

That didn't seem to Pray like much of a clue, but he nodded to keep Boles talking.

"The one man, he stuck a gun in my face and walked me backwards to the vault. The second one rushed past us, and I heard him tell Eugene not to press any button, or he'd die with his finger on it."

"What about the third man?"

"He ordered me to open the vault, which of course was where we kept the money after the armored car dropped it off yesterday."

"And you did."

"Open it? Damned right, with that spooky first man pressing his gun to my cheek." Boles went to rub the spot.

"Mary, the man who stayed on you, he never spoke?"

"No."

Pray always felt uncomfortable asking, much less repeating, the next question, but it was necessary. "And you don't know the race of that man?"

She shook her head. "Like I said before, they all wore masks and gloves, long-sleeved shirts and pants. But from the voices of the two who spoke, I'd say they were white, so I'm guessing two grains of salt didn't ask a peppercorn to join them."

Pray grinned, getting the impression Boles was trying to make him feel at ease for having to ask the question at all. People rarely behaved so considerately up north when probed by touchy questions.

"Anything else, Chief?"

"Yes."

"What?"

"Eugene."

"I had to send him home," said Mary Boles. "Poor boy was shaking like a leaf."

"How about Josh, then?"

* * * * *

"Mary has her habit of opening on time," said Josh Stukes. "I have mine of relieving myself just then."

Pray blinked at the doughy, fiftyish man with sandy hair. "You wouldn't wait till the first few customers came through?"

"Chief, you never worked in a bank around Christmas, let me tell you. There ain't never a time nobody's coming through the doors, so one time's as good — or as bad — as another."

"Give me the sequence again, then, as you remember it."

"All right." Stukes pointed toward the rear of the bank lobby. "I was just finishing, and the flushing kept me from hearing anything. When I opened the door, I got the muzzle of a Ruger forty-four stuck in my face."

"And you knew it was a Ruger..."

"...account of that's what I have next to my bed, for home protection."

Stukes pointed again. "This feller with the cannon walked me over to where they already had Eugene and Mary, kneeling on the floor, noses against the wall, and I joined them."

"And that was it?"

"Mary already had the vault opened by the time I got out there, and all I heard was the one feller telling us to all be quiet and nobody had to get theirselves shot. So I was quiet as a little mouse." Stukes suddenly grinned, but not pleasantly. "Speaking of mice, you gonna talk to Eugene again?"

Very evenly, Pray said, "Yes."

"Hope for your sake he changed his undies first."

* * * * *

"Chief, I really don't know what else I can tell you about that frightful experience this morning."

Lon Pray watched Eugene Cornwell cradle a small dog in his arms. The dog was a little mop of brushed hair and cute as a bug, the living room decorated tastefully even without the handsome tree and draped bunting of pine branches.

"Eugene, I won't know what'll help me either till I hear you tell it again."

Cornwell closed his eyes, then opened them. "Very well. I was behind my cage, just opening my cash drawer for the morning and arranging the currency and coins, as is my habit. Suddenly, I heard a stampede sound from the front door. I looked up to see these horribly dressed men barging past Mary, one stomping up to me and pointing a monstrous gun right here." Cornwell's index finger reluctantly left the dog and tapped the owner's forehead over his nose. "They say your whole life is supposed to flash by in front of you? Well, I swear my only thought was, 'Who would take care of Florinda?' Cornwell's finger returned to the dog, and his forehead dipped to touch the same spot on the dog, who licked appreciatively.

Pray waited a moment. Then, "You did hear the men speak?"

"At least one of—no, two of them. But I was too terrified to recall anything they actually said."

After striking out again on race, age, and idiosyncracies, Lon Pray concluded with, "Anything else you remember?"

"Yes," said Eugene Cornwell, "I remember that the reason I relocated here after college in Richmond was to be able to feel safe in a small town."

* * * * *

"That was still pretty brave of you, Luis."

Pray noticed that his words made the thirteen-year-old in the Atlanta Braves jersey stand a little taller, the wiry dog at his side whuffing.

"Without Mrs. Boles and her bank, we do not have our life here."

Pray knew that the Cortez family had moved in over the store they were running after Luis's parents had decided the migrant life left a lot to be desired. But he also knew how impossible becoming shopkeepers would have been if their loan request had been turned down.

"Luis, can you tell me again what you saw?"

"Sure thing. I am outside our store, washing down the windows from the dust that seems to come during the night from nowhere. I hear the sound of people running, so I turn to see three men crossing the street from the bank, guns in their hands but not shooting at anybody. I drop my window brush into the pail, and I wait until they cannot see me before I run after them."

"You get any kind of look at their faces?"

"Like I tell you before, they have masks over them, and gloves on the hands, too. But the way they run, I think they must be white."

"Why?"

Luis Cortez scuffed at the dust with the toe of his sneaker, causing the dog to stick his nose down there and paw the ground himself.

"Because they do not run so very well."

Pray tried not to grin this time. "Go on."

"I am coming after them down the path through the woods. I can hear them in front of me, making noise with their feet and hitting the branches with their arms, maybe, but not talking or nothing. Then I hear the sound of a car engine starting, only when I get to the edge of the fire road, I can see that it is a pick-up. By this time, though, the truck is too far away to see anything but that it is dark in color."

Which was what Pray had put out over the radio to his officers and the sheriff's deputies. Too bad half the vehicles in the county were pick-up trucks, and half of those were blue, black, or brown.

"Nothing else, Luis?"

The boy and his dog pawed at the ground in unison. "Just that when I tell my mother what I did, she slap me hard enough to loosen a tooth."

Chief Lon Pray tried to tell himself that, as a parent so close to Christmas, he wouldn't have done the same thing. Tried and failed.

* * * * *

"Anything?" said Pray.

Edna Dane, one of two uniforms on the roadblock, reached into her cruiser, a short pony-tail bobbing against her neck under the Stetson. Coming out with a clipboard, she looked down at it. "We've had fifty...five vehicles so far. Twenty passenger cars, three semi's, two buses, five panel trucks. The balance were pick-ups, seven of them 'dark in color.' We called them all in to Dispatch. None with more than two men in it, and no wants or warrants on any of the trucks or occupants."

Pray squinted past the other uniform, standing hipcocked with the butt of a riot pumpgun resting on his thigh. The pavement was otherwise empty in the noonday sun, people either working or doing holiday shopping at the mall ten miles away.

Dane said, "I'm guessing you haven't had any better luck at the other roadblocks or you wouldn't be here with me."

Pray turned to her. "You grew up in town, right?"

"Born and bred, except for four years of Criminal Justice over to the university."

"Answer me this, then. Three men hit our bank at opening, and then run for it instead of driving away. But they get into a pick-up on a fire road barely ten-feet wide that would leave them no way out if just one of our cars—or hell, a county surveyor even—happened to be on the road at the same time. Now, why would a gang risk that?"

Edna Dane smiled, and Lon Pray thought he could see the teenager she'd have been a few years back shining through. "I guess if I knew that, Chief, you'd have stopped fifty-five vehicles this morning, and I'd be worried sick over what you didn't find."

* * * * *

Chief Lon Pray stopped at his own house—a small ranch he rented on the edge of town—to let the dog out, as he did each day around lunchtime.

Everybody else in the area just seemed to let their pets roam free during the day, and probably, Pray thought, in time he would, too. But back in Boston, before making detective, he'd tried unsuccessfully to comfort one too many kids kneeling in streets, crying uncontrollably while they in turn tried to will their pets back to life after being hit by passing cars.

And Lon Pray didn't think he could tolerate that happening to Grizzly at this time in his life. In Pray's own life, that is.

After his divorce, most of the marital property—house, car, even their TV's—went to the ex- or her lawyer. Funny, Lon realized as he unlocked his back door. You thought of her as "Sally" in Boston but down here as "the ex-." I wonder if other guys—

Which is when Pray was knocked nearly flat.

"Grizzly!"

The combination German shepherd/Irish wolfhound had already bounded by him, loping around the yard like a race horse around its paddock.

Watching him, Pray couldn't stay mad. Grizzly had been the first creature in his life after the divorce, and the chief knew that, in a very basic way, the dog kept him sane.

By the time Grizzly got the pent-up energy burned off, Pray already had washed out his water bowl and filled it with fresh from the tap. Placing the bowl down in the yard, Pray watched Grizzly pad over in that slightly prancing way he had from the Irish side of his family. Lon decided to let the dog run free for another ten minutes, then grab a sandwich-to-go at the restaurant before wracking his brain again on why the robbers had planned their escape as they had.

And why the roadblocks hadn't turned them up.

But meanwhile, he'd take a page from Joe Bob Brewster's book and just sit on his porch, giving himself an early Christmas present by watching Grizzly enjoy the habit of midday exercise.

* * * * *

Driving by the Brewster place, Lon Pray gave a thought to stopping and asking Joe Bob a third time if he'd spotted anything, but the man was holding up a newspaper instead of the usual book, just the carroty hair visible above the top of the paper. Pray thought Joe Bob must be deep in thought, too, because he wasn't rocking, and Old Feller wasn't in his customary position but rather a full yard away from the chair.

It was five minutes later that Pray, ordering his trademark ham and cheese on wheat with mayo, suddenly registered what he'd seen. Then he put it together with what he'd heard, both as answers to his questions and as statements that had seemingly been offered gratuitously.

And, sprinting to his cruiser, Chief Lon Pray thought he'd figured it out.

* * * * *

Twenty minutes later, the man in the rocker was still holding the newspaper, and Old Feller was still lying a good three feet away. Which was fine by Lon Pray, now crouched behind a tree rather than sitting behind a wheel.

Pray waited for three minutes more, until he heard the shrill whistle from the back of the house. Then he leveled his Glock 17 and yelled over the sound of breaking glass. "Let that paper fall from your hands without lowering them!"

Old Feller looked first toward Pray, then to the rocker. The paper trembled, but didn't fall from the fingers holding it.

"Be smart!" yelled Pray a little louder. "Nobody's been shot yet. Don't make yourself the first."

From the back of the house Officer Edna Dane's voice rang out with,"Clear in the house. I say again, the house is clear."

Pray yelled a third, final time, "Last chance to see Christmas."

The paper then wafted down, the hands staying in the air and about even with the carroty hair and the face below it that was almost, but not quite, Joe Bob Brewster's.

Chief Lon Pray said, "Just a day of bad bio-rhythms, Earl."

* * * * *

"Chief, I was beginning to think I'd have to hit you in the head with a hammer."

Lon Pray watched the Santa coffee mug shake as the man holding it shuddered in his rocking chair. "You did everything you could, Joe Bob. It just took me a while to catch on."

"I mean, I lead with my brother, I flick my head toward the house, I even go on about Old Feller and 'strangers.' But all you do is kind of grin and drive off."

"Joe Bob, I just didn't get what you were telling me till I drove past half an hour ago."

"When my brother Earl was out here."

"Right. I'm guessing he wasn't too pleased with your mentioning his name to me."

"He thought he had a tight plan, all right," said Joe Bob, taking a slug of coffee. "Him and the other two hit the bank, then run down to the fire road. One gets in his own pick-up that they left there, the other runs with Earl almost to my place. Old Feller didn't kick up any fuss when his owner's brother happens to stroll around from the back and ask how I'm doing. Then Earl tells me that him and his 'friend' are gonna be in the house for a few days, waiting for things to cool down before they call their third friend to come back and pick them up."

"Along with the guns and the money."

"The money Earl never showed me, but he sure did wave that gun under my nose, and I knew I couldn't say anything direct-like to you, or he'd have shot through the window there and killed the both of us."

Pray said, "So you tried to tip me, Earl didn't like it, and he came out onto your porch here to impersonate you."

"Which was pretty smart of him, what with my habit of sitting out here." Joe Bob took another slug from the mug. "Only my book wasn't big enough to cover his whole face, so he had to use a newspaper, which I doubt you've ever seen in my hands. That was what tipped you, right?"

"That plus some other things. I wondered how out-of-towners would know about the mill money and the fire road. I also wondered why the third man in the bank never spoke."

"Simple," said Joe Bob around another sip of coffee. "Old Mary Boles might've recognized his voice."

"Another thing was, when I drove by a little while ago, your brother wasn't rocking in the chair like you do."

"Earl tried that, but his rhythm was all off, and he caught Old Feller's tail underneath."

"That's the last thing."

"What is?" said Joe Bob.

Pray gestured toward the sleepy hound. "Old Feller wasn't switching his tail under your chair, and that seemed to me oddest of all."

"Habits."

"What?"

"Habits," said Joe Bob Brewster. "We all have them. Sometimes they hurt, but sometimes they help, too.

Chief Lon Pray found himself nodding in time to Old Feller's tail.

✯ ✯ ✯

Fruitcake Cookies and Bringing Mother Back to Life

Special Feature
Non-Fiction

I stood at her kitchen counter chopping pecans while my sister rifled through the underneath cabinets between my legs in search of her industrial sized baking sheets.

"Oh, this will be such fun," she chattered, "baking fruitcake cookies with you for the first time in all these years."

I spread my legs a little wider and looked down at her. "What do you mean fruitcake cookies? These pecans are for my famous cocoon cookies. I hate fruitcake."

If I had been a man I would have been castrated with one sharp blow. Her head came up so fast and with such force I barely had time to step back and get out of the way. She turned to face me; her mouth gaped and her hands agitated the air from her position on her knees in the kitchen floor.

"Hush, hush your mouth. It's a sacrilege against everything good and holy to say such a thing. Baking fruitcake cookies the week before Thanksgiving is a family tradition. We will do it, and we will do it with the respect our fore-mothers set down for us all those years ago."

I couldn't respond for a few moments. I stood there with my butcher knife still poised in mid-air. Finally I said, "What planet are you from? I've never made fruitcake cookies in my whole life. And whose tradition? Our mother never had a tradition that included any kind of chunky cookie with disgusting lumps of candied fruit. We made cocoons, cookie press cookies, Daddy's favorite oatmeal chocolate chip with the chips replaced by red and green M&M's to make them festive, and of course, cut out cookies with silver ball decorations and Mother's buttercream icing on top. And the week before Christmas there is a whole 'nother list, but nowhere does a candied fruit figure into any of my family recipes."

Sissie's palm caught her scream. She bowed to the ground, almost weeping, like a female Dali Llama doing penance for a horrible sin. She whispered, "Mother failed you, pure and simple. I got married too young and left you to be raised by a menopausal wreck. She had me as a child, and you as an old hag."

"What are you talking about?"

"This, just this. You are my little sister and all you know about tradition is cookie press cookies and oatmeal chocolate chips. What else did she fail to teach you? Do you have good dental hygiene? Do you have a clue how to bake bread? How many pickles do you put up each year? Did you breast feed Mary Kate or was she a bottle baby? Oh, Lord, help me, I think I might fall out right here."

"I turned out just fine, I'll have you know. But I don't know who you are talking about. The only pickles my mother ever put up were Claussen's. They came from the refrigerated aisle at Kroger and they lived in our refrigerator, the middle shelf on the door. Wonder Bread contributed to these hips and Mary Kate did beautifully on Infamil, thank you very much."

I then worried if she might have been serious about the fainting part. The parenthesis around her mouth turned chalky and her eyes began to swim. I extended my hand to my overly dramatic sibling and helped her to her feet, realizing all the while that our living apart for so long had warped our sense of each other. She described family cooking traits and experiences that I had never known. How could that be? Was she going through some kind of emotional breakdown? Had our moving down here upset the usual rhythm of her life? Or maybe it was good that we were here. She had been alone for too long. She had raised two boys by herself after her husband's unfortunate death at such an early age. Maybe all that had bruised her more than I had ever realized before.

I led her over to the kitchen table and eased her into a chair. "It's okay," I said, patting her hand, "I'd love to learn how to make fruitcake cookies and I guess the reason I'm here is so you can teach me how."

She looked into my face, studying my infant crow's feet as if she had never seen me before. "Cornbread, you certainly know how to make cornbread. Tell me you do."

"Jiffy Muffin Mix," I whispered, feeling suddenly inadequate and out of sorts.

"Pound cake. Oh, tell me you know how to make pound cake."

"Duncan Hines," I replied.

"Spaghetti sauce?" Her eyes started to tear.

"Prego Traditional with mushrooms. It's good, honest it is."

"Please don't tell me you buy chicken stock in a can." A moan escaped her.

"Wyler's bouillon cubes," I admitted, looking down.

"Oh, Lordy. I'll have to start from scratch. But I've already raised my family. Hugh and Phillip have put up pepper jelly every year since Allen died. Does this mean I have to start all over again with you?" Her head lolled against the back of her chair, rolling back and forth like a pendulum of regret. She rubbed her face with arthritic hands; then she sat up straight as a wooden spoon and grabbed my shoulders so I could not escape. "You will learn the traditions of our heritage if I have to hold remedial classes from a nursing home. I will make it my duty that your precious little Mary Kate knows all the secrets of corn chutney and how to assure her angel biscuits are light enough to take flight if need-be. It may be too late for you to perfect the arts, but she is still young. There is hope for her."

I decided that it would not be advantageous at this point to put up a fuss. I nodded obediently and resumed my position at the counter with my butcher knife and the other nuts. Sissie dug out the eight pounds of mulit-colored candied fruit that she'd had stored in her freezer since ought-one. A slimy night this will be, I thought, stifling the urge to gag.

Sissie re-fluffed herself and took on her culinary duty with a gusto that would make "Just-tone Wil-sone" proud. She instructed me on the proper way to chop our six cups of pecans. I was doing it wrong, of course.

"How many cookies are we making here," I asked. "Is there any food left for the squirrels to store up?"

"We're making enough to feed the troops at Shiloh, and every living friend and relative our family has claimed since I was born. That is except for Uncle Fred on Daddy's side. I think Bill Ennis even takes a dozen or two to his grand-momma's grave instead of flowers each year. They're good, I'm telling you. People are depending on us, so start chopping or we'll be here all night."

"And people really eat these things? I mean, they don't use them as skeet or doorstops or anything like that, do they?"

I ducked as her hand whizzed past my head. She snatched a spoon from my hand at one point. "Just get your hands in there, Miss Smarty Pants, but be gentle. We don't want to wound the dough." Then she explained how to assure that our cookies had just the right amount of liquor to make them tasty but not so much that anyone would get soused.

"Liquor?" I said, perking up. With a shot or two of a decent libation, I might survive this night without committing murder or Hara-kiri on myself.

"Apricot Brandy," she replied, with a dignified nod.

Not my favorite, but at that point I would take anything I could get. At first she refused the offer of a sip, but before long we will both chugging the stuff, as well as licking our intoxicatingly doughy fingers. Our ornery chatter finally mellowed into giggles, which erupted without provocation and had us weeping and almost wetting our pants. By the time the tenth batch of cookies came out of the oven, we had sombered a bit and the topic of Mother came up again.

"I'm sorry your twenties were ruined by her death," she said, staring at her gooey hands. "She was not perfect, but she was the ultimate Southern mother, proud and dignified. She had a heart of gold and a spirit that soared with the birds."

"Yeah, but I guess having me at age forty must have clipped her wings. I was not exactly the perfect little Southern belle she'd expected. I've never been as socially entrenched as you are. I remember her experiencing the vapors on more than one occasion when I opened my sixties, flower-child mouth. Like the time I said the word Tampon at the dinner table. I thought she might expire into her pot roast right then."

"Oh, but Julia, you were perfect. You just grew up in a different age. You still are perfect in my eyes, even though you don't know how to cook. I wanted a baby sister more than anything in the world, and I prayed so hard and so long for you. God goofed the first two times with John and Arthur, but finally, for my thirteenth birthday, there you were."

It was my turn to tear-up now, and I let them roll. I had never heard sweeter words. My heart filled up so full I thought I might pop and rain candied fruit down on us both. When I composed myself enough to speak without spitting, I said, "I do wish Mother had taught me these things, though. Maybe I would like fruitcake cookies if I had been introduced to them early on."

"Oh, you <u>will</u> like fruitcake cookies before this night is done. But, I regret that we can't nip this whole cooking problem in the bud. If only I had Mother's recipe box. I could teach you every livin' thing you ever wanted to know. Gee, I wonder whatever happened to it? I guess Daddy sold it in the garage sale when he and his new hussy moved into their fancy new motor home. Ain't that just our luck?"

"You mean that old green tin box?" I asked. "The one stuffed with all those magazine recipes and scraps from yellow note pads?"

"That's the one."

Our eyes met. She knew what I was about to say, and it took everything she could do to keep from exploding into squeals before I got the words out.

"It is in my kitchen, in the cabinet over my stove."

"Go, go quick..."

The next thing she saw was my backside. My feet were out the door and hoofing it one house over. And I was back in record time, panting and holding the green tin box with all the reverence of the Holy Grail. I placed it on the counter in front of us, which Sissie had wiped clean in preparation of its arrival in her home. I let her do the honors of lifting the lid. We gazed at the crumpled papers and note cards living within it as if we were looking into the womb of the Holy of Holies. Sissie fingered the edges of our Mother's lifetime, and paused reverently before grasping one piece between her finger and thumb. She gave a tug.

Mary Horst's Fresh Coconut Cake. (That's our mother.)

We both "aah'ed" and tears welled up again. I removed the next jewel. *Aunt Bill's Fresh Apple Cake.*

We took turns ushering each recipe out of its tomb with all the fanfare we could muster without falling completely apart. *Aunt Willard's Angel Biscuits, Company Peas.* We blinked convulsively to clear our view. *Francis Stovall's To Die For Cheese Cake, Paula Ennis' Cranberry Orange Salad, Daddy's Favorite Shit on a Shingle, Eggs a la King* – no one claimed it, *Granny's Homemade Peach Ice Cream.*

Our mother was right there with us. We could taste and smell each delicacy as we removed it lovingly from the box. We read the titles aloud in a kind of litany to our family heritage and to the mother who we were certain was sitting across the kitchen table from us at that very minute. Sissie would pull a recipe and recite a memory to go with it.

"Oh, you weren't as big as a minute, probably six or seven years old at the most, and we had you propped up on the kitchen counter counting chocolate chips for this here triple-decker fudge cake. We told you it would be ruined and inedible if it had more than one hundred chips in it so you'd better count carefully or the whole birthday dinner would be a flop."

Even I got to share a few memories. Mother had cut up one of the first boxes to have the recipe for Rice Crispy Treats printed on its side.

"This is history," Sissie said, holding the scrap of faded cardboard up to the light. "Why, I think I might have an unopened box from that year stored in my attic. They changed their logo sometime right after that, you know. All those old packages and my collection of McCormick spice tins will be worth a fortune someday. You just wait and see." Sissie has the habit of being a major, big-time, pack rat, if you can't tell. I often wonder how many real rats have gotten major, big-time fat off all of her "unopened" antique dry goods.

By the time we had emptied our green memory tin, it was four a.m. We had sobered up and twenty-four dozen fruitcake cookies had been cooled, tinned, Christmas bowed and put away. Most importantly, we had revived a family tradition that will last for generations to come. Now, the week before Thanksgiving, we bake fruitcake cookies with my daughter - the same way Sissie did in her youth and the way I did vicariously through the rich stories she shared with me that night. And we always clear off a place at the kitchen table for Mother to sit and listen in. You see, I didn't miss out on anything growing up. No, I'm the little sister who has everything a little sister, and a daughter, could ever want or need - a mother whose legacy is alive and well, and a sister who loves me enough to teach me how to make cookies I despise.

* * * * *

My sister and I have been neighbors for several months now, and I have to say it is working out fine. I'm not sure why many family members and friends advised us against it. Maybe they had visions of sibling rivalry or familial unrest. But we'll have none of that. Sissie has fortified my pantry with the proper ingredients every Southern woman needs to create the masterpieces we unearthed from Mother's recipe box, and she has taught me the correct seasoning method for my set of new cast iron skillets. I've even fried okra. It's a real challenge to get those suckers brown and not slimy, and succeeding is an accomplishment I rank right up there with delivering my kids.

I suppose the reason for our mutual civility is our basic love for each other, or maybe it is because I consider her my elder, whom deserves my respect. More likely it is because we've lived and loved through miles of heartache and survived them. And even over the miles of highway that laid between us, we managed to be there for each other with loving support, long distance hugs and/or the occasional swift kick in the butt when that was more the order of the day.

Fruitcake Cookie Recipe

6 Cups chopped pecans
1 lb. white raisins
1 -8 oz. package dates
1 lb. Candied cherries
1 lb. Candied pineapple
¾ Cups flour (to mix with fruit)
1 stick oleo
1 ½ Cups light brown sugar, packed
4 large eggs
2 ¼ Cups flour
3 scant tsp. soda
½ tsp. cinnamon
1 tsp. nutmeg
½ tsp. cloves
5 Tblsp. milk
½ Cup apricot Brandy

Chop nuts and fruit well, then flour fruit and nuts with the ¾ Cups of flour. Set aside. Cream oleo and brown sugar well, then add eggs one at a time, beating well after each one. Sift dry ingredients, and add sugar mixture. Add milk and brandy. Add to this mixture the nuts and fruit and mix well.

Drop by tablespoons full onto lightly greased cookie sheet. Bake at 325 degrees for 12 to 15 minutes.

Sissie often doubles this recipe. I, on the other hand, avoid it at all costs.

✯ ✯ ✯

SandScript 2004

Emerald Coast Writers Membership Application

We are a 501-c-3 not-for-profit organization.

Please print and fill out the following membership application form and mail it, with the appropriate dues, to:

**Emerald Coast Writers, Inc.
PO Box 6502
Destin, FL 32550**

NEW MEMBER _____ RENEWAL _____

Name:_____ Date: _____
Address: _____
City: _____ State:_____ Zip Code: _____
County of Residence:_____
Country of Residence: (if not USA) _____
Company Affiliation/Occupation: _____ Work Phone:_____
Home Phone: ( ) _____ Fax ( ) _____
Email Address: _____
Do you have a web site? URL:
_____

Please attach a short bio and any information about yourself, your writing, or your company that you would like ECW to know.

Membership Desired:
Membership year is: March 1 - February 28 or 29. Pay half of appropriate dues after September 1. If paying after January 1, it counts for a full year. <u>All Fees must be paid in U.S. Dollars.</u>
   ___ $25 Florida Resident
   ___ $30 Affliate (non-FL Resident)
   ___ $35 Affiliate (outside US)

Signature: _____ Date: _____

General members will receive an invitation via email to join our private online email community on yahoogroups.com)

Corporate affiliations and sponsorships are available. Please contact us for more information. See our website for details: www.emeraldcoastwriters.org

Members of Emerald Coast Writers, Inc.

Emerald Coast Writers

POBox 6502, Destin, Florida 32550
www.emeraldcoastwriters.org

Members of Emerald Coast Writers, Inc.

2003-2004 Officers & Directors

Founder & President:	Julia H. Schuster
Vice President:	Phil Turner
Secretary:	Diane Harris
Treasurer:	Ellen Martin
Director, Education & Programs:	Janet Manchon
Director, Info. Technology:	Darlene Dean
Director, Literary Journal:	Sherry Marcolongo

Committee Chairs

2004 Writers' Conference:	Phil Turner
2005 Writers' Conference:	Joyce Holland
2004 SandScript Contest:	Tom Corcoran
2005 SandScript Contest:	Sherry Marcolongo
Historian:	Carol Anderson
Newsletter Editor:	Marguerite Hartt
Press Releases:	Judy Winn

Benefactor and Lifetime Member
Ms. Sadie Willett

Members
* Charter Member

Adams, Joe
Albert, Kyle
Altazan, Reg
Anderson, Carol*
Bakowski, Fred
Baroni, Lesly
Beith, Xellaine
Betts, Lee
Bonner, Bill
Bouchard, Jacqueline
Bowling, Lynn*
Brinkley, Ritch
Brown, Mary*
Bui, Chris
Cain, Bill
Campbell, Jan
Carpenter, John
Carter, Sarah Anne
Caster, Marvin
Christen, Hank
Christen, Lynne
Church, Mahala*
Compton, Randy
Coutu, Armand
Cox, Jerry
Crews, Deborah
Crowther, Gary
Dean, Darlene
Edwards, Audrey
Flowers, Lee (Jr.)
Forester, Nancy
Foster, Noel
Fraser, Anne
Frazer, Ron
Frederick, Wilma*
Gardner, Melita
Garzoni, Mary Heinz
Gasparian, Rusty
Germano, Charles
Grafton, Charlene

Guy, David
Hanna, Dee Dee
Harris, Diane*
Harrison, Marie
Hartt, Marguerite
Heath, Dale
Hill, Myra
Hinze, Ann
Hinze, Vicki
Hogeboom, Edward
Holland, Joyce
Howes, Pat
Husted-Brawley, Adrienne
Ilarraza, Carlos
Karian, Arlene*
Krueger, M.L. (Lou)
Lanier, Gray
Larson, George
LeCompte, Jennifer*
Lee, Jennifer
Lofton, Valerie*
Lutz, Susan*
Manchon, Janet
Marcolongo, Sherry
Martin, Ellen*
Martzy, Kinga
McInerney, Fucshsia
Meacham, Katina
Merrill, Delores*
Michel, Kenneth
Miller, Harold
Moyer, Jean
Mucci, Joan*
Nash, Randy
Neau, Michel
Noble, Judith
Paprocki, Alice
Petaccia, Mario
Powdermaker, Alan

Prater, Lon
Pusch, Millie
Rasor, Tonya
Riles, Melissa
Rogers, Robbie
Rosati, Amy Jo
Russell, William (Rev. Dr.)
Sassano, Beverly*
Saunders, Ellen
Saunders, Karen
Schoeppner, Kay
Schuster, Charles
Schuster, Julia*
Scott, Riotta
Sherrow, Charles
Shorter, Gail*
Shriver, Nancy
Snider, Susan
Stiff, Gil (Jr.)
Taylor, Monique
Treadway, Sherri
Turner, Philip
Vreeland, Maureen
Walker, Sue (Dr.)
Wendland, Audrey
Whitaker, Fred
Whitford, Jan
Wilcox, Betty D.
Willcox, Ray
Willett, Dale
Williams, Jerri
Winn, Judy
Winston, Bill
Winter, Barbara
Wood, Glenda
Woodfin, Stephen
Yoder, Michael
Yohe, Patty
Zerick, Lura

Published Authors of Emerald Coast Writers, Inc.

When our organization was first formed, we had no idea of the number of talented, professional writers that were looking for a "home." They are accomplished writers in their own right and are published across numerous genres, including fiction, non-fiction and poetry. Several contribute regularly to newspapers and magazines; some write for e-zines and support sites for writers. It is with great pride we showcase here some of our members who are published in book-length products.

Author: Mark Randolph Conte
Title: *IN THE ARMS OF STRANGERS**
Publisher: Gaius Press
ISBN#: 1591099528
Price: $22.95, 6x9 softcover
Genre: General Fiction
This is a grim, realistic look at the courts, lawyers and the whole criminal justice system. Not for the faint of heart. Distributed by Baker & Taylor

&

Title: *DELILAH & OTHER STORIES**
Publisher: Xlibris
ISBN #: 07388-6482-X
Price: $21.95, Regular softcover
Genre: Fiction
Main story is about four children who try to save the lamb, Delilah, from being their Easter dinner.

*Available on Amazon.com and BarnesandNoble.com

Author: Bill Bonner
Title: *RETURN TO CHASTITY*
Publisher: Jada Press
ISBN#: 1-9329-9301-0
Price: $15.95
Trade Paperback
Type: Mainstream Fiction
Synopsis: An FBI agent investigates a suspected terrorist who is a former fiancee. Terrorism, love and revenge touch the lives of innocent and guilty alike.

Author: Bonner DuLong
(Pen Name for Bill Bonner and Terri Dulong)
Title: *IMMORAL SYMPHONY*
Publisher: Gardenia Press
ISBN: 0-9744938-5-6
Price: $14.50
Trade Paperback
Genre: Mainstream Fiction
Two homeless people become involved with Project 1947 and find murder and conspiracy as part of an ominous secret.

Author: Charlene H. Grafton
Title: *DIAGNOSTIC AND PRESCRIPTIVE METHODS: A TEXT FOR TENNIS AND RELATED SPORTS*
Publisher: Winning Ways, Okla. City, Okla. 7/1/78
ISBN #: 571-249
Teaching methods to understand the difference between learning problems and learning disabilities.

&

Title: *TENNIS: STARTING OFF RIGHT-OR LEFT*
Publisher: Winning Ways, Okla. City, Okla. 7/1/1981
ISBN #: 908-889
A method of tennis instruction (The SOROL System) based on dominance.

Author: Marie Harrison
Title: *GARDENING IN THE COASTAL SOUTH*
Publisher: Pineapple Press
ISBN #: 1-56164-275-6
Price: $14.95, Softcover
Genre: Non-fiction
Marie covers flowers and plants for the Coastal South. She also discusses pesticide use, beneficial insects, exotic invasives, and gardening for birds and butterflies.

Published Authors of Emerald Coast Writers, Inc.

Author: Marguerite Hartt
Title: *THRIFTING INTO A DEBT-FREE, CAREFREE LIFESTYLE*
Publisher: Universal Publishers
ISBN #: 1-58112-602-6
Price $14.95, Softcover
Genre: Personal Finance
This book provides tips for saving on virtually all goods and services. It includes personal stories and clear, specific examples.

Author: Vicki Hinze
Title: *LADY JUSTICE*
    Book #2 in the Special Detail Unit Series
Publisher: Bantam Dell Publishing Group
ISBN #: 0553583530
Price: $6.50, Mass Market paperback original
Genre: Mystery/suspense. Thriller.
The Consortium, an international group of businessmen, launches a silent war against the United States using biological contaminates to destroy crops and create the need for medical technology it intends to black market.
&
Title: *BODY DOUBLE*
    Book #1 in the WAR GAMES series
Publisher: Silhouette Books
ISBN #: 0373513267
Price: $5.50 (paperback) Available in both hardcover & mass market paperback
Genre: Action/Adventure
Buried alive, Amanda West escapes her early grave. The Special Forces captain knew she'd been captured by the enemy while on assignment, but Amanda didn't understand where the mysterious IV wound on her arm came from, or where she'd even *been* for the past three months.

Author: Joyce Holland
Title: *MY, MY, MYRA*
   Sex, Lies, Money and Murder on Florida's Emerald Coast
Publisher: Author House
ISBN# 1-4107-2675-4
Genre: True Crime
Myra Vaivada regularly cruised the island in a limo to pick up men or women to feed her insatiable sexual appetite. Her husband Robert didn't mind, so what made her place a gun to his head and blow his brains out?
&

Anthology Title: *BLONDES IN TROUBLE & OTHER TANGLED TALES*
   Edited by Serita Stevens
   Story inside by Joyce Holland: *Eva's Eyes*
Publisher: Intrigue Press
ISBN# 1-890768-56-1

Author: Lon Prater
Title: *FROM THE BORDERLANDS*
Publisher of Book: Warner Books
ISBN# of Book: 0446610356
Price of Book: $7.99
This edition is softcover. Previously released in hardcover as BORDERLANDS 5.
Genre: Horror (Anthology)
Lon's story "Head Music" appears in this Stoker-winning anthology; his story received an Honorable Mention in the forthcoming Year's Best Fantasy & Horror.
&

Title: *MIDNIGHT IN THE NEW PROMISE*
Publisher of Book: Scrybe Press
ISBN#: 0974834068
Price: $3.99, Softcover
Genre: Fantasy (Industrial fantasy chapbook)
Imagine Tolkien's world moved forward to the Industrial Revolution, plus a gritty noir story line; that's the world of New Promise.

Published Authors of Emerald Coast Writers, Inc.

Author: C. G. Sherrow

Title: *GOORG-CHEE: A SCI-FI QUEST FOR FREEDOM***
Publisher: iUniverse
ISBN#: Hardback 0-595-76071-6   Paperback 0-595-29479-0
Price: Hardback $24.95
      Paperback $14.95
Genre: Science Fiction/Space Opera
A man wakes with no memory of his identity then joins forces with the diverse aliens sharing his predicament to escape the artificial environment.

**Available at Amazon.com, A1Books.com, BarnesandNoble.com, iUniverse.com or BooksaMillion.com

Author: Audrey K. Wendland

Title: *FLORENCE — the True Story of a Country Schoolteacher in Minnesota and North Dakota*
Publisher: Beaver's Pond Press
ISBN #: 1-59298-063-5
Price: $15 + S&H, Soft cover
Genre: Non-fiction
Live the adventures with seventeen-year-old Florence; her trials and tribulations bringing education to the Norwegian immigrants. A fun read for everyone.

Author: Lura Zerick

Title: *GETTING OLDER AND ENJOYING IT!*
Publisher: Infinity Publishers
ISBN#: 0-7414-2099-6
Price: $11.95, Softcover
Encouraging seniors to have a more fulfilled life.

&

Title: *THE GOLDEN OLDEN DAYS*
Publisher: 1st Books (now Authorhouse)
ISBN# : 1-4033-0789-X
Price: $9.50, Softcover
Genre: Memoir
Rural family lifestyle of '30s and 40s.

SandScript 2004 - Published Entries - by Author

Allen, Ronald H.	The Lean Acres Chronicles	63
Altazan, Reg	Last Thread	40
Altazan, Reg	Winter Swamp	1
Bouchard, Jacqueline	Justice Brings Me No Solace	18
Bouchard, Jacqueline	Too Old	83
Dean, Darlene	Friend	31
Dean, Darlene	Homeless	70
Frazer, Ronald	Kareem's Roti	44
Gardner, Melita	A Cat's Tale	79
Gardner, Melita	Drowning by Proxy	51
Gardner, Melita	Pop Culture Revisited	2
Gardner, Melita	That Palich Woman	9
Harrison, Don	November 22, 1963	43
Healy, Jeremiah	Habits	97
Krueger, Lou	Like Moses	59
Martin, Ellen	Tigra's Quest	32
Merrill, Delores	Sonya Renay Was in the Paper	78
Merrill, Delores	An Investigation of the Hermaphroditic Influence	88
Santo, Natasha	The Girl Who Was Afraid of Dogs	7
Schuster, Julia	Fear's Birth	17
Schuster, Julia	Fruitcake Cookies and Bringing Mother Back to Life	106
Scott, Riotta	The Old Woman's Song	72
Vreeland, Maureen	Something's Under the Bed	86
Wendland, Audrey	On Belay With Johnny	26

✯ ✯ ✯

Printed in the United States
22341LVS00006B/106-357